# PENLLERGARE

# A

# VICTORIAN PARADISE

Dedicated to all the members of the family.

# THE AUTHOR

Richard Morris is married to a member of the Dillwyn Llewelyn family and has been interested in John Dillwyn Llewelyn for many years. In 1977 he organised an exhibition of Llewelyn's images at the Fox Talbot Museum, Lacock and wrote an article for the *History of Photography* journal, the first time since Llewelyn's death that an exhibition of his work had been shown. Following that, he was involved with a programme on Llewelyn on S4C Wales and in 1980 was invited to put on an exhibition by the Welsh Arts Council. He has written many articles on Llewelyn and gained an MPhil at Brunel University in 1997 on Llewelyn, where he works in the Department of Design. He has also contributed an article on Llewelyn for the new *Dictionary of National Biography.* He is a past Chairman of the Historical Group of the Royal Photographic Society, of which he is a Fellow. He is a lecturer for the National Society of Decorative and Fine Art Societies, a member of the Scottish Society of the History of Photography, the Welsh Historic Gardens Trust, and both he and his wife belong to the Gower Society. He has also revived the calotype process as discovered by Henry Talbot and used by Llewelyn and other early photographers. He and his wife Sue have two children, two grandchildren, two springer spaniels, two tortoises and live in Buckinghamshire.

RIVER SCENE – PENLLERGARE. John Dillwyn Llewelyn.

# PENLLERGARE
# A VICTORIAN PARADISE

A short history of the
Penllergare estate
and its creator
John Dillwyn Llewelyn (1810-82)

by

Richard Morris

Published by The Penllergare Trust
1999

First Published (Hardback) 1999
Reprinted (Paperback) 2002


Copyright © 1999 Richard Morris


Published by
The Penllergare Trust
Coed Glantawe
Esgairdawe
Llandeilo SA19 7RT

ISBN  0 9536702 8 7


Printed in Wales by
Gwasg Dinefwr Press
Llandybie, Carmarthenshire SA18 3YD

# CONTENTS

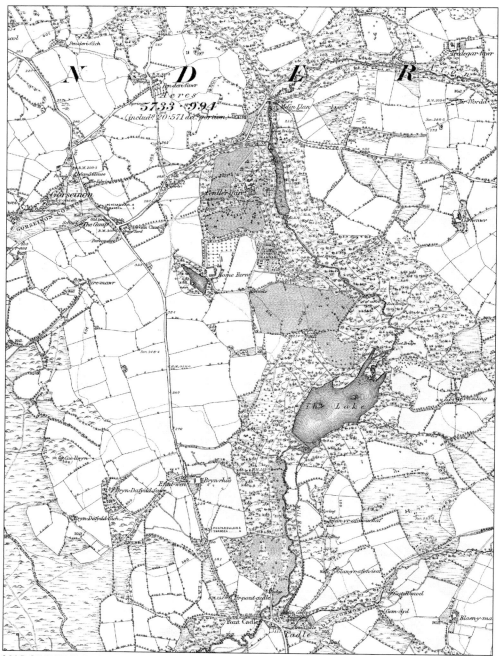

MAP SHOWING PART OF THE PENLLERGARE ESTATE, surveyed 1875-8.
From OS 6 inch First Edition, Glamorgan Sheet 14 (reduced).

# LIST OF ILLUSTRATIONS

# COLOUR ILLUSTRATIONS

# ACKNOWLEDGEMENTS

Over the years a great many people have become involved with my researches into John Dillwyn Llewelyn. The first were my mother-in-law, Mrs Olga Welbourn (née Dillwyn) and her daughter, now my wife, Susan, descended from John's brother Lewis Llewelyn Dillwyn. One cynical friend actually asked whether I had married 'for love or for the photographs' as my mother-in-law had a superb album of images, passed down the family, by John Dillwyn Llewelyn, Calvert Jones and others. Originally the album had been compiled for Bessie Dillwyn, Lewis's wife. The album now resides in the Victoria and Albert Museum in London.

In time, I came to meet the direct descendants of John and it is to them, especially the late Sir Michael Dillwyn Venables Llewelyn and his widow Lady Delia, that I am especially indebted for access to private family papers and photographs. Other descendants who gave me access to material were Vanda Morton, descended from Thereza Llewelyn, and the late Christopher Methuen Campbell who showed me some of his albums.

Others who deserve special mention are Colin Ford, former Director of the National Museums and Galleries of Wales, who invited me to research the negatives and other artefacts in their Llewelyn archive, then held in the Welsh Industrial and Maritime Museum; also Stuart Owen Jones, of WIMM and John Andrew, then responsible for the conservation of this archive. Dr David Painting, formerly of University College, Swansea, has helped with local information and in directing to me those seeking information on the family, especially in the case of Mr and Mrs Eady, who lived in the Lower Lodge, and accidentally stumbled across the remains of the Orchid House without realising the importance of their discovery. I still recall the day I went to identify the site and then slid down the steep slopes of the drive to get my first sight of the Waterfall.

Along the way there have been others whose help has been invaluable – Bob Lassam, the first Curator of the Fox Talbot Museum at Lacock, and the late Arthur Gill, first Chairman of the Historical Group of the Royal Photographic Society who I succeeded as second Chairman. Professor Margaret Harker Farrand kept encouraging me to continue with my interest in the calotype process and got me into the Library of the RPS before I finally became a member and ultimately a Fellow. As part of this journey there was the chance to organise an exhibition of John's work at the Fox Talbot Museum and, through the Arts Council of Wales, a major exhibition at the Glynn Vivian Gallery, Swansea, launched by the late Sir Cennydd Traherne in 1980. There also followed a programme on S4C Wales.

At Brunel University, where I work in the Design Department, I had the opportunity to study part-time for an MPhil on John Dillwyn Llewelyn. This, thanks to Professor Eric Billett, gave me the opportunity to dig out all those bits of information that I knew were hiding somewhere and yet needed time to be able to discover them. Even then time was somewhat at a premium and there are no doubt caches still hidden away, yet to be discovered.

Much probably vanished when the contents of Penllergare were auctioned in the late 1930s. I know both of Llewelyn's cameras were in that sale and I often wonder who has them now, perhaps not knowing their origins. I did, however, acquire a book on photographic chemistry that had come from that auction, signed by the author, Mr Hardwich, to John. And when I was let loose in the Cardiff archives I was able to identify both the stereo camera given to Thereza for her birthday and John's daguerreotype camera.

This present publication is due to Michael Norman who, when Trust Executive of the Welsh Historic Gardens Trust, was responsible for co-ordinating the initial efforts to highlight the importance of Penllergare to the heritage of Wales. Concern had been expressed at the fate of the Penllergare estate after a lease had been granted to develop parts of the site. I had first raised the issue of the Orchid House which is adjacent to the development and this concern then spread to the remainder of the estate.

Hopefully, both common sense and a care for the past will now take over, and where the developers have to carry out certain 'restoration' to the estate, this will be done in a manner that owes more to conservation than to the bulldozer. It is hoped this small book will alert people, especially those who live in and around Swansea, to the historic importance of what lies on their doorstep.

So my thanks are to Michael Norman for his tremendous enthusiasm in getting the project going and starting to canvass support for its objectives. As a result of a contact with Mr Geoff H Taylor it seems likely that a rhododendron, a hybrid named *Pengaer,* for which Sir John Talbot Dillwyn Llewelyn received an Award of Merit from the Royal Horticultural Society in 1911, but which had been thought to have been subsequently lost to cultivation, is actually still thriving in Valley Woods. This discovery again prompts the question, what more is to be discovered?

Thanks also go to Hilary Thomas who edited my original text and made it all look professional; to Donald Moore, one time Keeper of Pictures and Maps, National Library of Wales, former Chairman of the Glamorgan-Gwent Archaeological Trust, current Chairman of the Hafod Trust and a lecturer and writer on art and the landscape; and to Sir Harry Secombe, who, in opening an exhibition of Llewelyn's images at the Glynn Vivian Gallery in 1998, helped to bring Llewelyn's photographs and Penllergare to a wider public.

Many of the photographs and documents are still in family archives. In the public domain there are albums in the National Library of Wales, Aberystwyth, the Glynn Vivian Gallery, Swansea, and my mother-in-law's album is now in the Victoria & Albert Museum, London. The Royal Photographic Society, Bath, holds a number of prints. By far the largest public archive of prints and negatives, and some correspondence and equipment, is held by the National Galleries and Museums of Wales, Cardiff. Original letters, manuscripts and diaries, are in private archives.

Without money one cannot proceed. Very grateful thanks go therefore to those who have sponsored this publication. They are Bellway Homes (Wales Division) who, in 1999, are building on part of the estate, the Llysdinam Trust, the Ethel and Gwynne Morgan Trust, the West Glamorgan Archive Service and the anonymous donor of an interest free loan.

Finally, my thanks must go to my wife, Sue, who has had to put up with my filing system which seemed to explode all over our house. But without her I would probably never have heard of John Dillwyn Llewelyn.


Richard Morris
Long Gable
Cherrytree Lane
Chalfont St Peter
Bucks SL9 9DQ

1999



## YMDDIRIEDOLAETH PENLLERGARE – THE PENLLERGARE TRUST

The Trust, an independent company limited by guarantee (No. 4004593), a registered charity (No. 1082128) and publisher of this book, furthers the following objectives:

- the protection, conservation and restoration of the cultural landscape of Penllergare;
- the protection and enhancement of Penllergare's diversity of wildlife;
- the provision of an oasis in the surrounding urbanisation for free, quiet enjoyment by local people and visitors on foot;
- the promotion of knowledge and appreciation of Penllergare, its history and bio-diversity, and;
- sustainable training and employment (including volunteers).

Profits from the sale of this book will be devoted to the work of the Trust.

For further information, please contact the Trust Secretary at Coed Glantawe, Esgairdawe, Llandeilo SA19 7RT (telephone 01558 650735).

JOHN DILLWYN LLEWELYN. Self portrait *c.*1853. Notice the handkerchief across his knee possibly holding a connection to a shutter on his camera.

# FOREWORD TO THE FIRST EDITION

This book describes a remarkable designed landscape near Swansea – Penllergare – a locality particularly dear to the author. Latterly fallen into decay, the estate is still recognisable for its Picturesque qualities. Here is a 'local history' with many wider implications. At the centre of the story is a Glamorgan landowning family in its various ramifications, and the author has made skilful use of the family's papers and records, which fortunately survive in considerable quantity. The rare joy of the book is a treasury of illustrations produced by skilful artists and pioneer photographers. Several of the historic photographic images have become 'icons' of their kind, but most are unknown to the public. The author has added his own photographs to bring the imagery up to date.

Various themes run through the book, some made explicit in the text, others to be detected in the background. Undoubtedly the main theme is the creation of a beautiful landscape in the Picturesque style, a special ambition of landowners in the nineteenth century. They had the wealth to do so and sought to emulate their neighbours in adopting the latest fashion. Such landscapes were not simply a matter of planting trees and flowering plants; their layouts embodied philosophical and aesthetic principles and their realisation demanded exotic plants. They embodied a studied informality, a variety of content, a succession of viewpoints, and changes of gradient with surprises around every corner. Penllergare was an outstanding example of this kind of 'garden'. Various built features, both utilitarian and ornamental, were included. As well as the necessary kitchen garden, there was an orchid house and even an observatory.

Those responsible were landowners with business interests, but they were not content simply with possessing land. They were enthusiasts for art, antiquities and ancient buildings, and they supported societies which aimed to advance the state of knowledge. They themselves made learned contributions to different branches of science. Swansea was then a rapidly developing commercial and industrial centre, priding itself on its connections across the Channel to Bristol and beyond. In 1848 it attracted a meeting of the British Association for the Advancement of Science, which actually paid a visit to Penllergare to witness an experiment in using electricity to propel a boat on the lake.

One occupant of Penllergare, Lewis Weston Dillwyn, was an eminent naturalist and a Fellow of the Royal Society. His son John Dillwyn Llewelyn, became a pioneer of photography, and left an incredible visual record of the estate. Members of the family, especially the ladies, were accustomed to record the scenes around them in watercolour drawings, and numerous examples survive to complement or confirm the photographic record. Such skill was not unique to Penllergare. At Coedriglan, near Cardiff, Charlotte Louisa Traherne was an accomplished watercolourist, as was Charles William Mansel Lewis of Stradey Park, Llanelli, and Lady Catherine Allen of Cresselly, Pembrokeshire.

There is a moral at the end of this tale, for all is not well with Penllergare today. The house, the focus of the estate, was lost many years ago, blown up as a military exercise after falling into ruin, and its site is now a car park. Modern roads have constricted the site, and more houses, all very necessary, are being built in the locality. It is to be hoped that new development will not obliterate the beauty of the old landscape, but be planned so as to incorporate the best of the old for the benefit of the future.

The publication of this work is symptomatic of the present surge of interest in historic gardens in Wales, generated in large measure by the Welsh Historic Gardens Trust, founded as recently as 1989. The author, the editor and the Friends of Penllergare are to be congratulated on bringing this account to the notice of a wider public.


DONALD MOORE
formerly Keeper of Pictures and Maps at the National Library of Wales.

THE SUMMER EVENING. The Upper Lake, 25 August 1854.
Collodion image by John Dillwyn Llewelyn.

THE OWLS OAK – PENLLERGARE by
John Dillwyn Llewelyn. 1850s.

# PENLLERGARE – THE FORGOTTEN ESTATE

A few miles northwest of Swansea, and within sight of the motorway, lies what should be one of Swansea's great assets. Here, away from the noise and fumes of the passing traffic and encroaching development, one can enjoy the sound of birds, delight in the profusion of wild flowers, discover evidence of exotic plantings and a grand design. Here at Penllergare, astride the Afon (River) Llan, are the ravaged but still discernible remnants of an important historic landscape.

If John Dillwyn Llewelyn, the creator of the Penllergare[1] landscape, approached his estate from Cadle today, he would find it hard to discover the main entrance, yet it is still there, together with the Lower Lodge designed by Edward Haycock,[2] the Shrewsbury architect, c.1836. So too is the driveway up to the mansion, a feat of engineering construction that even many years of neglect cannot conceal. The lasting value of Penllergare is that it was conceived as a whole rather than as a series of segments. The mansion stood on high ground looking down over the valley, the river and the lakes. Though the gardens in front of the house have long vanished and the whole estate is now overrun with bracken and alien trees, it still retains the outline of the original plan. The paths can still be found weaving their ways through the woodlands, and on a rainy day many of the small rivulets still flow, as can be seen in the old photographs. Undoubtedly, John Dillwyn Llewelyn created his estate to follow the natural terrain of the ground, rather than fighting against it. This, for many, is the beauty and cleverness of his design, in a style now known as the Picturesque.

If one enters the estate from the top end (near the old Midway Café), the first attraction to greet the eye is the remains of the Upper Lake, or Fishpond as it was sometimes referred to. The upper end of the Lake has been lost by the construction of the motorway. However, a visit to the original Penllergaer Park (near the motorway service station), will easily reveal how the river meanders through woodlands that were once a part of Penllergare estate. There is even a white building that may be the very same one that features in the photographs by John Dillwyn Llewelyn, or if not, it appears to stand on much the same spot.

Although the Upper Lake is now somewhat smaller than it was originally, the islands shown in watercolours and photographs of the 1850s have been reconstructed in the last few years, and it is easy to see what it must have looked like in the days of the Llewelyns.

Walking on, the next feature is to the right, a flight of stone steps leading up to a plateau faced with stones. Here are more survivals[3] from the past, one of which is a small grotto into which water entered from above, whirled around and then went down a pipe and into the Upper Lake. Behind the plateau are the remains of paths leading to the site of the mansion.

One of the best features of the estate is the Waterfall, entirely man-made and dating from the 1840s when John Dillwyn Llewelyn constructed the Upper and Lower Lakes. Here nothing seems to have  changed.  One can even imagine that the trees are the very ones in photographs taken by John Dillwyn Llewelyn and his friends. This is a construction of quite outstanding design with a main fall and lesser falls coming in from the side. A tribute to the early workmen, as well as to the quality of Victorian engineering, is that the original sluice gate still works. When the Upper Lake was being drained recently, prior to being cleaned out, the water was diverted via the old sluice which runs on the far side of the Waterfall.

Down from the Waterfall the stream runs under a bridge. Alas, not the original Old Stone Bridge, but a modern construction, though the remains of the original bridge may be seen underneath its successor. But for this twentieth-century intrusion, the scene is almost as it is in the 1850s photographs.

If the visitor then looks to the right, the main drive from the Cadle end passes the quarry, where much of the stone for the estate buildings was dug, carried on a stone bridge. Though John's camera did not record this particular feature, the watercolour brush of one of his daughters, Emma Charlotte, has left a record of this quarry

Returning to the river which now passes through dense woodlands, where old paths can still be discerned, one reaches the Lower Lake. Originally, where the river entered the Lake stood the Boathouse, a chalet-like structure whose picturesque appearance is captured in John Dillwyn Llewelyn's photographs. All that now remains of this building are the stone footings. The Lake itself is now empty. It originally covered nineteen acres of impounded water held in place by a remarkable stone dam at the lower end. A sluicegate controlled the water. The dam still stands, as do a series of tunnels, part of the system to control the water level of the Lake which once abounded in trout and otters.

THE DRIVE FROM CADLE in 1991. Photographs by Richard Morris.

STEPS IN THE WOODLANDS, unearthed 1992.
Photograph by Richard Morris.

STONE STEPS LEADING TO THE TERRACE, unearthed 1991.
Photograph by Richard Morris.

If one turns one's back on the Lake and looks upwards towards the new housing estate, here, to the left, is the part of the estate known as Nydfwch, the site of a former house, vanished even in the days of John Dillwyn Llewelyn. However, there then still abounded masses of snowdrops, a sign of a former dwelling. Further up, towards the main dual carriageways from Swansea to the motorway, may be seen a large clump of trees to the right of the new housing estate. This is the area of the former Kitchen Garden and the Walled Garden containing the Orchid House. The stone wall is still standing, surrounding a more formal area once laid out with beds and paths. To one side of the wall are a series of ruined buildings, the former bothy and hot houses for melons and other exotic fruit.

Of the Orchid House only the stone walls remain, held together by the roots of trees. Inside is the cistern that held the warmed water and, at the top end, the waterfall, fed by water from the Home Farm pond through the coal-fired boiler to provide the heat. This is one of the very earliest stoves specially designed for the propagation of orchids. In later years, probably during the residence of Sir John Talbot Dillwyn Llewelyn (1880s-1920s), it was used for growing camellias, and two specimens still stand guard at the entrance.

At Penllergare some of the earliest experiments in photography and horticulture were carried out, and through the former we can get more than just a glimpse of the grandeur of the estate along with images of a wide variety of trees and plants. These images date from the earliest days of photography, as far back as 1840, and cover a period up until the late 1850s.

Through the photographs of John Dillwyn Llewelyn, his family and friends, we are, today, still able to appreciate the glory that was Penllergare.

# LOCAL INTELLIGENCE

## *GLAMORGANSHIRE.*

MARRIED.—On Tuesday last, at Penrice, John Dillwyn Llewelyn, Esq. of Penllergare, in this county, eldest son of L. W. Dillwyn, Esq. M. P. for Glamorganshire, to Emma, youngest daughter of the late Thomas Mansell Talbot, Esq. of Penrice Castle, and sister of C. R. M. Talbot, Esq. of Margam Park, also M. P. for the county of Glamorgan. The ceremony was performed by the Rev. Henry Strangeways, who came from Exeter for that purpose. The altar of the church was tastefully decorated with arches of flowers, as were also the gates of the churchyard; and carpets were laid over the path leading to the church. The bride, who was dressed in white lace over satin, appeared most interesting and lovely, and at the termination of the sacred ceremony, the happy couple set off for the mansion of Mr. Llewellyn, at Penllergare, amidst the tears and blessings of the neighbourhood; and the mingled feeling of sorrow for the loss, and prayers for the happiness, of this amiable and excellent young lady, rendered the day one of peculiar interest. Liberal distributions were made of clothing and dinners to the poor, and Swansea and the neighbourhood were enlivened with *feus de joie*, the ringing of bells, and every other form of rejoicing.

Report of the marriage of John Dillwyn Llewelyn to Emma Thomasina Talbot. 1833.

PIC-NIC ON GOPPA. September 1855.
Collodion image taken for Emma's birthday
by John Dillwyn Llewelyn.

## THE FAMILIES

Penllergare, which had been in the ownership of the Price family for over two centuries, came into the ownership of the Llewelyn family at the end of the eighteenth century. Early in the nineteenth century it passed, through marriage, to the Dillwyns.

The barrister, Gryffydd Price, last of his line, by his Will dated 7 June 1783, left his entire estate at Penllergare to his cousin John Llewelyn of Ynysygerwn, in the Neath valley. His son, Colonel John Llewelyn, inherited both estates but, as he left no male heir to succeed him by his wife Fanny, the estates passed through his natural daughter, Mary Adams, to Lewis Weston Dillwyn in trust for his son John.

Lewis Weston Dillwyn was the eldest son of a Quaker, William Dillwyn, who returned from America during the War of Independence. His diary for the period recalls obtaining passes from both the British and American armies. Having finally settled in England, William married Sarah Weston, the daughter of William Weston of High Hall, Walthamstow, in Essex, on 27 November 1777. Sarah was his second wife, his first, Sarah Logan Smith, having died in America in 1769. By his first marriage William had a daughter Susanna. By his second there were three sons and four daughters.

The Dillwyn family had resided in Pennsylvania since the end of the seventeenth century when William's grandfather, also called William, had fled 'with his friend William Penn' from England and persecution. This William is said to have been involved with the planning and layout of Philadelphia. His grandson was a businessman with property in Bermondsey, Brighton and also possibly in Holland. On one of his visits to Wales he had been shown over the old Cambrian Pottery at Swansea. Why he later decided to purchase the lease is unknown. The eldest son of Sarah and William Dillwyn, Lewis Weston, was born in London in 1778,[4] and in 1802, whilst working at his maternal grandfather's cooperage business, was sent to Swansea to take charge of the Pottery.

7

Lewis Weston Dillwyn settled at The Willows in Swansea, and in 1807 married Mary Adams, the illegitimate heiress daughter of Colonel John Llewelyn of Penllergare and Ynysygerwn. How Llewelyn came to meet Mary's mother, Sarah Adams, remains a mystery. She later married a Mr Beazley and is probably buried in St Mary's, the collegiate church[5] close to her brother's residence in the High Street, Oxford.

Lewis Weston Dillwyn holds an important place in the history of Swansea. Though his immediate family had resided in America for three generations, his antecedents in Wales possibly included the Welsh bard Ieuan Deulwyn,[6] appointed by Edward IV in 1462. Though without any knowledge of ceramics manufacture, Dillwyn soon settled into his new job with enthusiasm and during his tenure produced some of the very finest pottery ever made in Wales.

As a wealthy businessman and landowner he took his place in local politics and, as well as sitting on the magisterial bench, served as Sheriff in 1818. He sat on many committees concerned with welfare and health, and was especially concerned with the reform of miscreants who were detained in the House of Correction. From 1835-40 he served as an Alderman and Mayor of Swansea and was given the Freedom of the Borough. In 1834 he stood for, and was elected to, the First Reformed Parliament where he strongly supported Welsh affairs. During his time in Parliament one of the major Bills to come before the House was that for the Great Western Railroad as it was then called. Though he voted in its favour, he wrote in his Diary on Monday 10 March 1834 'I think it rather a Humbug'. Before he retired from Parliament in 1841 he was offered a baronetcy to oppose the Tory interests in the county, but he declined to accept it.

Lewis Weston Dillwyn was one of the founders, and first President of the Royal Institution of South Wales. In 1848 he was one of those who welcomed the British Association for the Advancement of Science to their first ever meeting in Swansea. For this event he produced *The Flora and Fauna of Swansea*, a copy of which was given to each of the delegates.

Six children were born to Lewis and Mary Dillwyn. Their first child was Fanny (1808-94) who married a notable archaeologist Matthew Moggridge. Next came John (1810-82) followed by William (1812-19) and Lewis Llewelyn (1814-92) who married Bessie de la Beche. Two further children were 'little' Mary (1816-1906) who married the Revd Montague Earle Welby, and Sally (1818-28) whose deathbed scene was painted by C R Leslie.[7]

John, the eldest son, was born John Dillwyn on 12 January 1810 at The Willows, Swansea. His earliest years are largely unrecorded as it was not until 1817 that his father began his Diaries recording both the domestic and public activities of the family. At the age of nine John began his education under a series of tutors. On 13 September 1819 the first of these, Henry Knight, a nephew of Colonel Knight of Tythegston, came to spend a few days at Penllergare prior to his appointment. Dillwyn recorded in his Diary that day that the Revd Bruce Knight[8] informed him that:

THE DILLWYN LLEWELYN CHILDREN. September 1854. Collodion image taken for Emma's birthday by John Dillwyn Llewelyn.

a Treaty which he has negotiated is completed and that Mr Henry Knight will under-
take the education of my dear John as a private tutor. My object is to possess him
with general knowledge, gentlemanly manners and good principles, rather than
make him a walking Lexicon, and Mr Knight, besides being an excellent classical
scholar appears to unite all the requirements.

Unfortunately, a few years later, in 1822, Dillwyn was forced to act hurriedly:

> Tuesday 4th June - This morning my dear Mary was obliged to complain to me of
> Mr Knight's conduct which she has hitherto at the expense of her own health and
> comfort concealed from my knowledge and which occasioned my great
> astonishment. He appears before she was thirteen to have tried to inveigle Fanny
> into a marriage engagement and so persuaded her that so long ago as last August
> she told her mother of his strange behaviour. Mary relying on his promises kept the
> matter secret but he has lately renewed his persecutions of Fanny by repeated
> attempts to kiss her, and by the most unjustifiable attempts to set her against her
> mother and by treating the latter with the grossest insolence when she spoke to
> him about it. I found an immediate separation to be unavoidable.
> Wednesday 5th June - I had last night offered to Mr Knight the use of one of our
> carriages to take him home this morning, but it was found that he had left the house
> in the night and gone home. With his strange temper I had long borne, under the idea
> that he was of service to our dear John and it was this feeling which induced Mary
> so long to conceal his mis-conduct from me, with a reliance on his honour that it
> would not be repeated. He claims a promise which Fanny made before she was 13
> of always continuing to be his friend and at that time she declares she did not
> understand his meaning, and has grossly abused her mother for attempting to
> enforce this absurd and childish engagement. I charitably think him mad.

John's final tutor was Henry Moule of Melksham[9] who settled in Dorset, entered the church
and remained a lifelong friend.

Upon coming of age, and entering into his Penllergare and Ynysygerwn inheritances, John
assumed the additional surname of Llewelyn in accordance with the terms of his maternal
grandfather's Will. On his twenty-first birthday, 10 January 1831, he received a twenty-one
gun salute in Swansea. In 1832 he undertook the Grand Tour of Europe, an almost obligatory
event for young gentlemen of the time, ending up in Christiana, now Oslo, during a cholera
outbreak, which delayed his return home.

In 1833 John Dillwyn Llewelyn married Emma Thomasina Talbot, the youngest daughter of
Thomas Mansel Talbot of Penrice and Margam and Lady Mary (née Fox-Strangways). By
this time Emma's father was dead and her mother was married to Captain Sir Christopher
Cole. Both Sir Christopher and Lady Mary were delighted with the match, and for John it
gave him a personal link to Emma's cousin William Henry Fox Talbot of Lacock Abbey. [10] The latter

was already known to the Dillwyn family as he had spent some of his teenage years at Penrice with his Talbot cousins and corresponded with Lewis Weston Dillwyn on botanical matters.

John, like his father before him, became actively involved with local affairs. In October 1834 he qualified to act as a magistrate for the county of Glamorgan and in 1835 was made High Sheriff of the county. In those days the life of a magistrate was rather different from what it is today. In 1843 South Wales saw the Rebecca Riots, an explosion of unrest amongst the working population against the toll gates. As a magistrate John, armed with his pistols, would join the local militia to try and stop the burning of the gates. He was present at Pontardulais when, for the first time, some Rebeccaites were actually caught. They were later sent for trial in Cardiff and John was present at the trials in his capacity as a magistrate. For his efforts at keeping the peace, during which he was wounded, the Secretary of State, Home Office, Sir James Graham, personally commended him for his bravery.

In the 1830s John Dillwyn Llewelyn was a regular competitor in the Swansea and Neath Horticultural Society exhibitions. His principal competitor was John Vivian of Singleton, and so frequently did they take the top prizes that for a while both offered to withdraw. However, they were eventually persuaded to continue competing. Many of John's prizes were for orchids grown in his stove, a heated greenhouse, at Penllergare. John also took a great interest in the cottage gardens of his tenants and other local inhabitants.

Many of the local good causes, such as the Swansea Infirmary, Swansea churches and clothes for the poor, could claim John as both a benefactor and member of their committees. He regularly helped those less fortunate than himself with personal support and donations. But John Dillwyn Llewelyn was a man of strong principles and his support for a good cause was, on occasion, tempered by criticism. In 1876 he greatly upset the Swansea School Board, of which he was a member, by accusing them of wasting money on the wrong kind of education under the Elementary Education Act. Perhaps his most memorable phrase from his Letter to the Rate Payers of Swansea, summed up his feelings - 'You cannot keep a starving child with nothing but a grammar to comfort him.'

One of John's most lasting benefactions was the donation of forty-two acres of his estate at Knapp Llwyd, now called Parc Llewelyn, near Morriston, in 1874. Parc Llewelyn was formally opened on 3 October 1878, but ill health prevented John from attending the opening ceremonies. His own desire had been for the least possible publicity. Only in a letter to Sir Joseph Hooker, dated 21 October that year, did he reveal that the Parc Llewelyn gift had cost him twenty thousand pounds. Asthma had plagued John all his life and in his later years prevented him from always taking part in public life, though he still retained his place on local committees.

The arrival of photography in 1839 saw John at the forefront of activities which led to the foundation of the Photographic Society of London in 1853, and he became a founder Council Member of what is now known as the Royal Photographic Society. Through photography he was able to leave a fascinating record, not only of his estate, but also of members of his immediate family.

John and Emma's first child, Thereza Mary,[11] was born at Penllergare on 3 May 1834. Her grandfather Lewis Weston Dillwyn commented in his Diary on 5 May:

> Received the glad tidings of our precious Emma's safe delivery ... and of my having become a Grandpapa tho' I don't much fancy the title.

Thereza developed many of the interests of her father and was an enthusiastic photographer, botanist and astronomer. On 13 August 1857 she married Nevil Story Maskelyne of Basset Down in Wiltshire. Nevil was a young Oxford don, an early photographer, comparatively poor but madly in love with her.[12] Thereza communicated with many of the botanists of the period including the Hookers[13] and both George and Mrs Bentham[14]. It was to Bentham that she sent a query about a bittercress *(cardamine hirsuta)*, and he read her paper on it to the Linnean Society. Thereza died in 1926 at her late husband's home at Basset Down.[15]

The second child, John Talbot, was born at ten in the morning on Thursday 26 May 1836, at Sketty Hall where the Llewelyns had gone during rebuilding work at Penllergare. He met the full approval of his grandfather Dillwyn who wrote the following day in his Diary '... a fine whacking fellow he seemed to be.'

John Talbot, often referred to as Johnny or Jack, was educated at Eton and Christchurch College, Oxford. He became High Sheriff of Glamorgan in 1878, was created a Baronet in 1890, was Mayor of Swansea in 1891 and represented Swansea in the House of Commons 1895-1900. His botanical interests led to him being made a Vice-President of the Royal Horticultural Society. On 7 May 1861 he married Caroline Julia Hicks Beach, daughter of Sir Michael Hicks Beach, a former Lord Chancellor.[16] Apart from one of his daughters, Gwendoline, Sir John was the last of the Dillwyn Llewelyn family to live at Penllergare.

The third child, Emma Charlotte, was born at Penllergare on Saturday 11 November 1837, the year of the succession to the throne of the young Queen Victoria. Neither a photographer nor an astronomer like her sister, she was an accomplished water colourist and has left a number of sketches of Penllergare, the colour of which add to the reality of her father's photographs. Following her marriage to Henry Crichton in 1863, they moved to Clyro in Herefordshire where they became friends of the Revd Francis Kilvert. Kilvert's first curateship was under the Revd Richard Lister Venables, whose daughter Katherine Minna married Charles Dillwyn Llewelyn, a son of Sir John's and added the surname Venables to those of Dillwyn and Llewelyn.

The year 1838 was an eventful one for the family. William Mansel Dillwyn Llewelyn, Willy as he was known, was born on Tuesday 25 December. John's brother Lewis became engaged to Bessie de la Beche the daughter of the geologist Sir Henry de la Beche; Emma Charlotte was christened; John's sister Fanny Moggridge gave birth to a son; the Queen bestowed the title of Royal on the Institution of South Wales; and in July Henry Talbot visited Wales to stay with his cousins at Margam and Coedriglan and also visited Penllergare. Willy died on 29 March 1866. During his short life he had been a friend of Theodore Talbot of Margam with whom he shared many experiences, not least their time at Oxford. Following university he had joined the 4th Hussars, spending some time in Ireland, and was a Lieutenant at the time of his death. The same year, 1866, Bessie, wife of Lewis Llewelyn Dillwyn, also died, aged only forty-six.

The final three children of Emma and John were all girls. Sybella was born at Penllergare on 17 January 1842, a day when the thermometer stood at 36 degrees and there was a white frost. The event was somewhat of a surprise to the family as Lewis Weston Dillwyn recorded in his Diary:

> As it was not expected till next week the news of our dear Emma's safe delivery of a Girl much surprised us ...

Alas, their joy was not to last. By Monday 31 January there was serious concern over the health of the new baby, and in the early hours of Friday 4 February she died.

Elinor Amy was born on Wednesday 10 January 1844, a Leap Year, and was baptised on 15 February. Like her sisters she was interested in sketching. She appears to have suffered ill health, causing her father considerable concern in his last years. She died, unmarried, in 1887. The last child born to Emma and John was Lucy Caroline who arrived on 1 July 1846. She was probably born slightly crippled and was constantly seeking treatment. She was an amateur artist of some considerable talent, travelling to mainland Europe with a companion to paint and sketch. Lucy died in 1920 and, like others in the family, is buried in the churchyard of the family church at Penllergaer, then called Gorseinon.

Towards the end of his life John spent more and more time in London. Perhaps he was able to escape the asthma that had plagued him for much of his life. During these periods his son, John Talbot, looked after matters at home and by the 1870s was living at Penllergare.

In 1871 John and Emma were seeking a house in London and that year they moved to Cornwall Gardens. In 1879 they purchased Atherton Grange in Wimbledon leaving their son and daughter-in-law at Penllergare in complete charge of their Welsh affairs. John's continuing interests in horticulture led him to take Mr Nunns, the head gardener at Penllergare, with him to Wimbledon.

Emma died at Atherton Grange on 19 April 1881 and was buried 'at John's church at Gorseinon' as his brother Lewis wrote in his Diary. Emma's death caused John a great deal of grief. His letters home were full of doom and gloom. Sometime the same year he wrote to his son Johnny:

> I am just able to leave my bed and crawl across the room to sit in an arm chair - but

am still very weak and ill. The news on all sides appals me - it reads like the early chapters in the French revolution. What can I do for the protection of your sisters.

A short time later his spirits were still embittered. He wrote again to Johnny referring to the success of young William, Johnny's son then at Eton:

> I am very glad to hear of Willy's success & I pray God that he may grow up to be a blessing to you - there is nothing more bitter than the ingratitude of children. I am sorry to say that we got on very poorly.[17] Nelly [Elinor] as is the worst of convalescent invalids is very fractious and wilful - she seems to take a pleasure in thwarting me in all ways and insists on running foolish risks in this cold weather. I feel responsible for her safety. So far my strength permits me - but the long solitary evenings which I have to pass are telling in evil guise on my mind & body.
> The gout I suffer from is proverbially said to make its victims irritable - Since your poor mothers death every thing goes wrong & my only wish is to go to her - pray God soon.
> I have no comfort, no prospect of any on this side of the grave - and then - what then?[18]

John died on Thursday 24 August 1882. and was buried alongside Emma in the churchyard of their family chapel on the estate. Despite the ravages of the years and the best attempts of vandals, his lasting memorial remains the grand landscape at Penllergare.

Almost as soon as he had inherited Penllergare, John had begun his ambitious programme of improving not only the house but also the landscape. Family connections had brought him into contact with Henry Fox Talbot of Lacock Abbey who, in addition to being a pioneer photographer, was also an enthusiastic gardener. He and John exchanged both specimens and advice. John's marriage to Emma Thomasina Talbot also brought him into close contact with Emma's mother Lady Mary Cole. From their letters one can easily imagine Lady Mary and Mrs Dillwyn gossiping about gardening and from this, and his own contacts with such horticultural giants of the period as the Loddiges of Hackney, one can assume that John received much help and advice.

The young bridegroom determined that Penllergare would be transformed for his bride and family, and in this grand scheme improved access was a priority.

THE DRIVE FROM CADLE. *c.*1852.
Calotype by John Dillwyn Llewelyn.

## *THE DRIVE*

The first major work to be carried out by John at Penllergare was the construction of the Driveway, of a mile and a half in length, from Cadle up to the mansion, and the building of a Lodge. The work involved was immense, necessitating the carving out of the rock face and the building up of the roadway to make a drive wide enough for the family carriages. It also involved the destruction of the Old Mill at Cadle. Today there stand an impressive pair of modern gates, installed by the bj group in the 1990s, beyond which, on the left hand side, is the restored Lower Lodge designed by Edward Haycock.

The first reference to the new road is found in the Diary of Lewis Weston Dillwyn for 17 September 1832. He wrote that 'we [John & himself] walked up the line of his intended New Road from Cadley,' an expedition they repeated three days later.

John and Emma were married on Tuesday 18 June 1833, and whilst on their honeymoon in Europe they received news of work in progress at Penllergare in letters from their family at home. John's brother Lewis was able to write to him in Geneva on progress on the road in a letter dated 7 August 1833:

> The road I think is getting on very well, the stones are put on from Cadley side of the Primrose Meadows to about half way through Nidfwch wood.

A somewhat more anxious letter reached John in Venice in August from his parents. Their news regarding the decoration of the house was satisfactory but as far as the work on the road was concerned, somewhat worrying. His father wrote:

> I wish I could give as satisfactory an account of your new road. I cannot help

thinking that you would have preferred a little Hill rather than having the Wall so very much raised, but as I have always been accused of old fashioned prejudices on this subject I am afraid of giving any directions - and often wish you were here to judge for yourself - - there is still an immense quantity to fill - Lewis tells me that all the new Road as far as the Nedfwch wood is stoned.

By 14 September the news was much happier and John's father was able to write:

I went all over your new Road a week ago which appears to be altogether well done & it may be completed in readiness for you and your better half to landscape on your return to Penllergare.

A mad dog bit two of the labourers working in the road but they apparently suffered no harm. Lewis Weston Dillwyn recounted the episode in his letter of 3 November 1833 to John:

Neither of your other two Laborers who were bit by a mad Dog on the new Road have yet suffered from their disaster but some of my Sheep are said to have died Mad, & it is supposed were bitten as the Dog was seen in the direction of the Field where they were - numerous other mad Dogs have been killed in the Neighborhood & all dogs by public placards are now ordered to be kept either muzzled or tied up.

On their return from honeymoon Emma was taken along the road by John and she was able to write to her mother-in-law, Mrs Dillwyn, then staying temporarily at Burrows Lodge,[19] whilst waiting to move into Sketty Hall:

I have been able to see the road and was carried all the way by Fanny's poney, very pleasantly. John led me all the way and I admire it exceedingly.

A description of the road and its surroundings appears in the *Journal of Horticulture and Cottage Gardener* written by Mr Andrew Pettigrew of Cardiff who visited the estate in 1886, four years after John's death, when his son John Talbot Dillwyn Llewelyn was in residence. It vividly evokes the grandeur of the landscape:

The residence of J T D Llewelyn, Esq., stands on one of the finest sites for natural beauty that could be found in the county of Glamorgan. The elevation is some 300 feet above the level of the sea. The house, a commodious building of two storeys, commands extensive views from all sides, embracing rock, wood, water, hill and dale, and rich pasture land. The principal entrance to the demesne is a mile and a half from the Cockett station on the Great Western Railway, and about four miles from the town of Swansea. The private approach is a mile and a half in length. It is conducted through the park and along the breast of a wooded hill, and cut out of the solid rock in many places. As it ascends the hill the scenery increases in grandeur till the house is reached. On the left the ground rises a considerable

MARY DILLWYN. Miniature possibly by Thomas Baxter.

LEWIS WESTON DILLWYN. September 1841. Daguerreotype taken in Cheltenham.

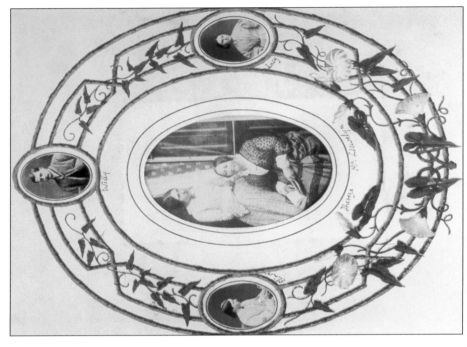

THE DILLWYN LLEWELYN family, from a carte-de-visite album compiled by Emma Charlotte Dillwyn Llewelyn.

height about the drive, and on the right it descends far down to the valley, where flows the river Llan, a rapid trout stream, which passes through two lakes at different levels as it winds its way through the picturesque grounds of Penllergare on its course to the sea. The banks on both sides of the valley are covered with heavy timber, principally Oaks, in the best of health, while here and there large trees of Hemlock Spruce (Abies canadensis), Taxodium sempervirens, Wellingtonia gigantes, and Cryptomeria japonica stand out in bold relief, lit up in many places by a glorious undergrowth of the best species and varieties of Rhododendrons and hardy Azaleas, some of which are of large dimensions and in the most luxuriant health, the soil and situation being favourable to their growth.

Mr Pettigrew, who was gardener to the Marquis of Bute at Cardiff, goes on to say:

As the house is neared the scenery becomes still grander. The valley narrows and deepens, and the drive for some distance runs close to the edge of a precipice, with only a frail rustic wooden rail between the road and it for protection; or, what is more reasonable, to mark the edge of the cliff, which descends perpendicularly 100 feet or more below the road. The view from this point, looking to the right over the tops of the trees and down to the bottom of the glen, is charming. The ground from the foot of the precipice sweeps boldly down to the river, and then rises rapidly to a great height on the opposite side, completely shutting in the view. The view from the left side of the road is hemmed in by the rock out of which it is cut, and the rising ground above it.

At one time a series of lodges, occupied by members of the estate staff, were passed as one drove up from Cadle. All but the Lower Lodge have vanished. Above the Lower Lodge, the wooden gateway is a replacement for the original structure shown in an early photograph by John. Here, on Friday 23 April 1841 a potentially serious accident occurred which Lewis Weston Dillwyn recorded in his Diary for the day:

In descending the Hill near the Middle Lodge the Pole broke and we were only saved from destruction by the skill and great exertions of Lewis. The Horses galloping and kicking at last dashed the Carriage so as to break it in pieces against the Gate Post by the Lower Lodge and we were miraculously thrown out as not to be seriously injured.

The North Lodge also survives but is now divorced from the estate by the dual carriageway, to the motorway, from Swansea. Hardly noticed, unless you were to slide down the bank, is the stone bridge carrying the road over the quarry. This structure, built for the weight of horses and carriages, was capable of carrying the weight of heavy road-building machinery during the preliminary stages of recent construction work. The top end of the roadway is now cut off by the boundary fence of the new buildings that replace the mansion. However, the boldness of the scheme is still very much in evidence.

UPPER LODGE. *c.*1852. Calotype by John Dillwyn Llewelyn.

THE BRIDGE CARRYING THE ROAD OVER THE QUARRY. 1991. Photograph by Richard Morris.

THE DRIVE ABOVE THE LOWER LODGE. *c*.1852. Calotype by John Dillwyn Llewelyn.

THE ENTRANCE TO THE DRIVE AT CADLE. *c*.1852. Calotype by John Dillwyn Llewelyn.
The Lower Lodge is on the left. These are the gateposts into which the carriage dashed
and was wrecked on 23 April 1841.

Cadley Mill about the year 1829

THE OLD MILL AT CADLE. Destroyed when the new road was made. *c.*1829. Artist unknown.

PENLLERGARE. *c.*1852.
Calotype by John Dillwyn
Llewelyn.

## THE HOUSE AND ESTATE

Penllergare was the home of the Dillwyn Llewelyn family from 1817 until 1936 when Gwendoline, the daughter of Sir John Talbot Dillwyn Llewelyn who had died in 1927, moved out of the house. By that time Sir John's son Charles was married to Katherine Minna Venables, the co-heir of the Revd Richard Lister Venables, and had moved into his wife's house at Newbridge-on-Wye, in mid-Wales.

Penllergare had been in the hands of the Price family from at least the sixteenth century, though there is no evidence as to what the house looked like at that period. At the time of the Civil War, the then Squire Price was an ardent Royalist supporter. Lewis Weston Dillwyn in his *Contributions towards a History of Swansea* tells a story about this Squire Price that he had heard from Colonel Llewelyn:

> The late Colonel Llewelyn told me of a tradition which he heard as a boy, that on the first arrival of some Parliamentary troops at Swansea, a party was detached to Penllergare, with orders to bring Mr Price, dead or alive, to the Commander, and they were instructed to look out for a man on a certain kind of grey horse, which Mr Price always rode. As the owner had taken good care to get out of the way, one of the party thought fit to steal  this favourite horse, and being seen when riding off in disguise, the soldiers fancied that Mr Price had escaped from some hiding place, and by a bullet killed their comrade in his stead.[20]

At the beginning of the eighteenth century, *c.*1710, a new house of three storeys was built and *c.*1800 Colonel John Llewelyn employed the Guernsey architect, William Jernegan, who added a two-storey extension with exterior canted bow windows.[21] It was probably this building that Benjamin Heath Malkin,[22] in 1803, described as a 'new house in good style, not far removed from magnificence.' Watercolours, probably by members of the Dillwyn family, show us what this building looked like. There is also a more formal, but probably more accurate, drawing by C R Leslie.[23]

The succession of the house and estate from the Prices to the Llewelyns can be traced in the Wills of both Gryffydd Price and Colonel Llewelyn. That of Price is dated 6 June 1783 and includes the following clauses:

> To and to the Use of my Cousin John Llewelyn of Ynisygeron in the County of Glamorgan Esquire his heirs and Assigns for ever I give and devise unto my said Cousin John Llewelyn my Capital Mansion House and Demesne Lands of Penllergare with the above mentioned Six closes of Arable Land formerly part of the Tenement of Nydfywch aforesaid but from henceforth to constitute part of and be occupied with the said Demesne And all other its Rights Members and Appurtenances And also all and singular other my Estates whether Freehold or Customary Freehold or otherwise (which said Customary Estates I have surrendered To the Use of my Will except the Messuage or Tenement of Lands called Trewiddfa ycha alias Tyr y wch lawr Heol as herein after is mentioned situate lying and being in the Counties of Glamorgan and Carmarthen or in either of them of every Tenure whatsoever with all and singular their Rights Members and Appurtenances To hold to and to the Use of him the said John Llewelyn and the Heirs Male of his Body.[24]

The Will of Colonel John Llewelyn states:

> This is the last Will and Testament of me John Llewelyn of Penllergare and Ynis Ygerwn in the County of Glamorgan Esquire. If I die at Penllergare my wish is to be buried in Llangwelach Church in a private manner attended by six or eight Friends as Bearers ... I give devise and bequeath all and singular my Real Estates whatsoever and wheresoever and of what nature of kind soever whether Freehold Copyhold or Leasehold and whereof I am seized possessed or entitled unto, whether in Possession Reversion or Expectancy together with their Rights Members and Appurtenances unto William Williams of Abergwin in the County of Glamorgan Esquire, John Jones of St Helens near Swansea in the same County Esquire, Lewis Weston Dillwyn of Swansea in the said County Esquire, my Daughter Mary Dillwyn the wife of the said Lewis Weston Dillwyn and my Wife Fanny Llewelyn, To hold the same Estate according to the respective tenures and qualities whereof unto and to the use of the said William Williams, John Jones, Lewis Weston Dillwyn, Mary Dillwyn, and Fanny Llewelyn, their Heirs Executors Administrators and Assigns, But nevertheless upon Trust that they do so soon as

conveniently may be after my Decease by such good and effectual Conveyances and other Assurances in the Law as Counsel shall advise, settle convey limit and assure all and every the same Estates in manner following, that is to say, Upon trust in the first place to permit and suffer my said wife to occupy and enjoy rent and tax free during her Life (except in the meantime one of my Grandsons or Granddaughters, hereinafter mentioned, shall happen to attain his or her age of Twenty one years, and be entitled to the Possession of my said Real Estates under or by virtue of the Limitations hereafter directed to be thereof limited and created, All that my Mansion House at Penllergare with the Appurtenances ...

The remainder of the Will continues to list the various other properties that were consigned to the care of the trustees. During the years of the trusteeship, Lewis Weston Dillwyn made many astute purchases on behalf of the estate and his eldest son and, by agreement with neighbouring landowners, bought and sold parcels of land so as to tidy up the boundaries of Penllergare. In 1878 the acreage in Glamorgan owned by John Dillwyn Llewelyn amounted to 8797 acres. In addition he owned 3587 acres in Breconshire and 2483 acres in Carmarthenshire.[25]

Dillwyn's life was not made easy at times by the non-family trustees, especially Mr John Jones of St Helens. His Diary entry for Sunday 14 December 1817 shows his impatience with the man whilst endeavouring to obtain probate for Colonel Llewelyn's Will:

> Yesterday in a meeting of several Gentlemen at Gibbins Bank, John Jones of St. Helens, so far forget himself as to use words which occasioned me this morning to send the following remonstration in a letter to his excellent Brother in Law Richd. Phillips who was then staying at his House. 'Tho I can hardly believe he meant it yet the words which Mr Jones addressed to me clearly implied a Threat of giving me trouble in my Trusteeship unless I joined his proposed party against Mr Sockett & as his remarks, however unintentionally offensive were made in a public Company they have necessarily converted my former wish into a firm determination to remain perfectly neuter - Any private advice or assistance from Mr Jones would be always gratefully received but I cannot submit to an influence (especially in public) that I must not consult or invite to Penllergare whoever I please & rather than yield to such an idea I would remain in Chancery till Doomsday.

In a further Diary entry for Thursday 1 January 1818 Dillwyn wrote:

> Went with Mary in the Carriage to sign a power of attorney for Lewis Thomas to act on our behalf in proving the will at a Manor Court in Neath, & for which Mr. Wm. Gwynn had very unnecessarily obliged me to bring a Witness to Mr. Ll's signature from London - In the Streets of Swansea Mr. Jones of St. Helens on the subject mentioned at page 27 [16 December] called me so many Billingsgate names and behaved so outrageously that I determined to horsewhip him if he did not give me

proper satisfaction - I kept myself quite cool till the Blackguard called me a Liar - New Years Day - fine weather.

Dillwyn quite clearly had severe problems with this trustee and the following day, in his Diary, he informs us that Mr Jones had 'openly quarrelled with almost or quite every other Gentleman in the neighbourhood.'

When Lewis Weston Dillwyn resigned from the Pottery and prepared to move into Penllergare it was in the belief that there was sufficient money from the estate of Colonel John Llewelyn to keep up the family's existing lifestyle, but such expectations proved false.

The last days of the Colonel are recalled by Lewis Weston Dillwyn in the Appendix to his Diary for 1817:

> Mr [sic] Llewelyn on his return from London on Friday the 20th June came to spend a few days with us at the Willows and at his arrival looked extremely ill. On Monday the 23rd he went to Penllergare... as he fancied that the country air would expedite his recovery and next day on my going over to see him I thought him better... Mary & I on Saturday the 28th drove over in the gig expecting to spend a pleasant day at Penllergare and on our arrival we found him sitting on the stone by the pillar at the front door and looking extremely ill. Leaning on my arm ... he told me he was certain he had not many days to live and desired me to have all done that could be done to mitigate his sufferings and not again to leave him. He then besides his keys gave me the money which he had in the house... He often desired me to get his will but Mrs Llewelyn objected and the Doctors forbid me to let him talk long on matters of Business... he obtained my promise to give Mrs Llewelyn the Willows in exchange for Penllergare he represented both to Mary and me the provision which he had made for us to be much larger than we afterwards found it. Among other things he particularly told us we should immediately have 300 a year for John and 250 each for Fanny, Willy and Lewis and that when they arrived at 17 the allowance would be encreased to 500 for the eldest and 400 each for the two younger boys and 300 for Fanny. He said we should find he had given us enough to support Penllergare if we chose it "in splendor" or otherwise to save large fortunes for our younger children and it was under this wrong impression that I promised to retire from Business and to exchange my residences.[26]

In 1817 Lewis Weston Dillwyn and family moved from The Willows, Swansea, to Penllergare. The house into which they moved was old, rambling and damp, with a leaking roof and walls running with water, and was badly in need of restoration and improvement. Only when John Dillwyn Llewelyn entered into his inheritance were major improvements carried out. With John's coming of age in 1831 and his marriage to Emma Thomasina Talbot in 1833 it was time for Lewis Weston and Mary Dillwyn to consider the purchase of their own property as, by agreement with Colonel Llewelyn, his widow Fanny had moved into The Willows.

AT THE DOOR OF THE CONSERVATORY, PENLLERGARE. *c.*1852.
Calotype by John Dillwyn Llewelyn.

SOUTH FRONT, PENLLERGARE 1858. Collodion image by John Dillwyn Llewelyn.
Front left: Elinor Llewelyn, Miss Southern (governess), Annie Franklen, Jane Franklen,
Emma Llewelyn, John Mandre (gardener), Mrs Moggridge, Lucy Llewelyn,
Mrs Franklen, Mrs Lewis Dillwyn. Note the camera in the porch.

After deliberation, the Dillwyns chose Sketty Hall in Swansea, but before they could move into their new home it required alterations for which they employed the Shrewsbury architect, Edward Haycock.

In 1836 John Dillwyn Llewelyn began extensive alterations to Penllergare and the family moved temporarily into Sketty Hall, the home of his parents. He too employed Edward Haycock who, after a thorough survey, recommended the pulling down of the old three-storey building and renovating the newer part built by Colonel Llewelyn. A comparison of the old and new Penllergare house can be made through the early photographs of John and the watercolours by members of the family. Haycock's rebuilding and improvements transformed Penllergare which now became a comfortable home for the family.

An important addition to the house was the Conservatory, with heated pipes running underneath the pierced wrought iron floor that ran along the middle of the paths. There are a few photographs of the interior taken by John Dillwyn Llewelyn and by James Knight, who was tutor to the Llewelyn children. A detailed written description comes from Mr Andrew Pettigrew of Cardiff when he visited the estate in 1886:

> The conservatory, a substantially built half-span roofed structure, is slightly curved in its length to suit the wing of the building to which it is attached. It is about 60 feet long, 20 feet high, and broad in proportion, with a fountain and beds in the centre, and a narrow stage at the side of the path round the back wall. The wall is covered with Camellias and Orange trees, and the bed in the centre of the house is planted with large Camellias, Tree Ferns, and other greenhouse plants. Fuchsias and various climbers cover the rafters in front, and hang down in graceful festoons. The house contained a general collection of greenhouse plants, which were clean and healthy, and everything looked neat and orderly. Besides the plants in the conservatory the entrance hall of the mansion was neatly furnished with a miscellaneous collection of flowering plants, amongst which were a batch of well-grown plants of the extra fine strain of Calceolaria

Photography in the earliest days required a great deal of sunlight and long exposures. It is therefore rare to find interior photographs from these years. John made only two such photographs, both of the Library, but towards the end of the century Sir Thomas Mansel Franklen, a son of Emma's sister Isabella, made some interior photographs. There is also a watercolour, probably by one of the family, of the Round Room designed by Jernegan.

Most of the descriptions of the house come either from the family letters or from Emma's housekeeping books which recall such events as sweeping the chimneys or yellow washing the walls. Details of the interior after John's death are more easily found but are not relevant to the present study. The house is long gone and there will be few who now remember its interior, since it is almost sixty years since the last Llewelyn lived there.

Top: PENLLERGARE. *c.*1852. Calotype by John Dillwyn Llewelyn.
Bottom: PENLLERGARE RUINS. 1980s. Photograph by Richard Morris.

After the death of Sir John Talbot Dillwyn Llewelyn in 1927, the house was left in the care of his unmarried daughter, Gwendoline Harriet Llewelyn, with a reduced staff both indoors and outdoors. After she had moved out, a three-day auction was held in October 1936 of the contents of the house not required for the new property in mid-Wales where Sir Charles Dillwyn Venables Llewelyn was now living. Miss Llewelyn died on 2 January 1944 at her home in Bryn Road, Swansea.

The house and what remained of the estate was leased by the Bible College of Wales and later acquired by Glamorgan County Council. Neither of these organisations was able to carry out any plans for its upkeep. During the Second World War, Penllergare was occupied by the troops of General Omar Bradley and was very severely vandalised. Finally, in 1961, as an exercise for the Territorials of the Royal Engineers, the house was blown up in a series of weekend exercises under Major Attwood. He informed the *Swansea Evening Post* for 9 January 1961:

> The remains of the house will be demolished in three sections. The charges on the first section will go off at about 9.30 on Sunday morning. The timing of the other charges will, of course, depend upon the time taken in ensuring the safety of the personnel by the removal of the masonry and other precautions. We hope the final charge will go off at 3 to 3.30 in the afternoon.

And all that remained was a large heap of rubble. Happily, prior to the demolition the Round Room was removed to the family's new home in mid-Wales, as were some of the fine panelled doors.

The main core of the estate was later repurchased by Sir Michael Dillwyn Venables Llewelyn and currently it is leased for housing development and a 'country park'. In 1980 the then Lliw Valley Council purchased the area occupied by the house and Observatory and built new Council Offices. Within this area, which is now owned by the City and County of Swansea, stands the Observatory.

LIBRARY AT PENLLERGARE. 1850s.
Collodion image by John Dillwyn Llewelyn.

THE FRONT HALL, PENLLERGARE. 1890. Photograph by Sir Thomas Mansel Franklen.

PENLLERGARE. Probably taken 13 March 1843. Daguerreotype by John Dillwyn Llewelyn.
The Daguerreotype image is normally laterally reversed but this image is reproduced the right way around.

THE OBSERVATORY, PENLLERGARE
undergoing restoration 1981. From a
colour photograph by Gerry Lacey.

## THE OBSERVATORY

The Observatory is one of the few remaining original buildings dating from the days of John Dillwyn Llewelyn.

Both John Dillwyn Llewelyn and his daughter Thereza were keen amateur astronomers. John was a member of the Royal Astronomical Society, though their surviving records seem only to recall his recurring problems with his bank in paying the annual subscription. Such was Thereza's interest in astronomy that John built an Equatorial Observatory for her near the house. No doubt Thereza's interests in astronomy and photography were of particular relevance when she met her future husband Nevil Story Maskelyne, for he was the grandson of an Astronomer Royal, an Oxford don and an early photographer.

In the Diaries of Lewis Weston Dillwyn there are a number of references to observatories. The astronomer, Sir James South,[27] was a friend of Dillwyn who recorded visiting South's observatory in London in the late 1830s. On Sunday 14 June 1846 Dillwyn records a specific visit to 'Mr Jenkins Observatory in Wind Street' in Swansea. There are other references to telescopes and on Saturday 12 September 1840 Dillwyn, writing at home in Sketty Hall, recalled that 'Miss D & I amused ourselves for a short time by putting up the new Telescope which Sir Js South has sent me.' In 1851 the Llewelyns visited the Great Exhibition in Hyde Park, and in her letter to Mrs Dillwyn, Emma wrote that 'John longs for Rosse's great telescope.'[28]

On Monday 7 July 1851 the Dillwyns went to Penllergare and that day Lewis Weston Dillwyn wrote in his Diary that he went to 'Attend my dear Theresa [sic] in laying the first stone of the new Equitorial Observatory.'

Thereza wrote to her father who was away from home at the time at the meeting of the British

Association for the Advancement of Science in Ipswich:

> I laid the foundation stone of the observatory today, July 7th. When Grandpapa and Grandmama were here on Saturday we told them about it and they were very kind as to come over here today to see the first stone laid: so we went in procession to the place: they had got some stones ready and after I had laid the first stone, Emma laid the 2d, and Elinor the 3rd - which she was very delighted to do.

Dillwyn's comment in his Diary hints that there might have been an earlier building or at least a permanent telescope of some kind. Though no evidence survives to prove that this was the case, there was the telescope at Sketty Hall which may have been more than just a hand-held instrument. In the Diary entry for Tuesday 25 January 1842 Dillwyn wrote:

> Drove with Capt Smyth to Penllergare & retd [to Sketty Hall] to Dinner. ... The Evening cloudy & not favorable for the telescope.

Sometime around 1852 John made a calotype image of the building encased in scaffolding.

The Observatory is an Equatorial Observatory and it was here c.1857/8 that John and Thereza made some collodion photographs of the moon. In some brief memoirs written by Thereza when she was an old woman she recalled the event, though at this stage her memory was not always totally accurate:

> About 1855 he (my father) made a photo of the moon, and as moon light requires much longer exposure it was my business to keep the Telescope moving steadily as there was no clockwork action. That photograph was one of the first ever made of the moon. In 1869 a photograph now historical and described as being taken "at a time when the art of photography was in its infancy" was made by Sir David Gill, and is now at the Royal Astronomical Society London.

Thereza's Journals[29] of the period add a few further details and help to date the moon images to at least 1857 or 1858. The first relevant Journal entry is 12 January 1857 when she wrote that 'I had the camera fastened on to the end of the telescope.'

Next day she wrote that '... in the evening I went with Papa to try the telescope-camera, and we found that it did not answer as it was.'

On 20 January she wrote:

> I got D Mandre[30] to refasten the Thermometer, which had got loosened in the storm, & to alter the Telescope-camera; & when it was done I showed him & his son, "Venus".

OLD PENLLERGARE before the alterations. Watercolour. Artist unknown.

PENLLERGARE GARDEN FROM THE HOUSE.
Watercolours by Emma Charlotte Dillwyn Llewelyn.
Top: June 1860
Bottom: 1864.

PENLLERGARE INTERIOR. Watercolour by a member of the family.

THE ROUND ROOM, PENLLERGARE. Watercolour by a member of the family.

The next reference is not until 3 August:

> After I got home I made a good photographical experiment, and at night we went to the observatory, but we only saw A aquilae - as it clouded over after we had been there a short time.

This is the last entry referring to the Observatory and unfortunately there is no Journal for the following year so the exact dates for the images remain a mystery.

Amy Dillwyn, the youngest daughter of John's brother Lewis Llewelyn Dillwyn, was equally enthusiastic about the new telescope. In her private Diary she wrote:

> I looked through Uncle John's big telescope and saw the moon which looked like Gruyère cheese and also saw Jupiter and three of his moons; the fourth was eclipsed by himself. Harry and I returned to Hendrefoilan by moonlight.[31]

Grandfather Dillwyn was also an enthusiastic star gazer, and in his Diary for Wednesday 3 December 1845 he recorded this heavenly phenomenon:

> Day stormy but beautifully star light in the Evening. At ½ past 8 we were called by the Servants from the Drawing Room to witness something remarkable in the Heavens & found a magnificent luminous arck [?] extending over the zenith from the NE to the SW or thereabouts. It lasted about ½ an hour & in all respects exactly answered to the description of one seen at Buxton in 1774 as described in the abridged Trans: of the Royal Society Vol 16 p 627.

After the departure of the Llewelyns from Penllergare decay set in and the Observatory was not spared. The structure probably remained intact until the occupation by the American troops during the Second World War when it appears that the walls were used for target practice.

In 1980, when Lliw Valley Borough Council purchased the land to build their new offices, the importance of the building was eventually recognised and some restoration work was carried out, including a new roof for the telescope building. At this time, when questions were being asked as to the importance of the building, the Royal Commission on Ancient and Historical Monuments in Wales became involved and an investigator with the Commission, Mr Douglas Hague, wrote:[32]

> ... I am too busy just now to write at length, but there are some rum features about the building. The tiles are very odd; the only mention I have ever found is this [sic] German one! For a dark-room it had a big window, but that is what I assumed the room was intended to be.

The room attached to the actual Observatory was almost certainly used as a darkroom.

THE OBSERVATORY UNDER CONSTRUCTION. 1851-2. Calotype by John Dillwyn Llewelyn.

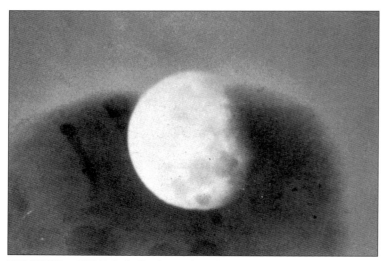

THE MOON. *c.*1856/7. Collodion image by John and Thereza Dillwyn Llewelyn.

Around the Observatory was a garden:

> Entirely devoted to the culture of the rarest and choicest florist flowers, [it] is laid out in small oblong beds for minutely observing the plants and flowers at all stages of their growth. Besides these and rockeries, it contains a great many pits and frames for growing rare and tender varieties. The large collections of Auricula, Carnation, Primula, Pansy, and other florist flowers grown here can scarcely be surpassed, if indeed equalled, in any private place in the kingdom. What is called the new garden adjoins this, and is partly enclosed by large shrubberies. It is a delightful piece of undulating pleasure ground tastefully laid out and planted with the choicest kinds of trees and shrubs. Amongst coniferous trees were good specimens of Cryptomeria japonica, Thuiopsis borealis, Cupressus Lawsoniana, Wellingtonia gigantea, Araucaria imbricata, Hemlock Spruce, and many others, ranging in height from 30 to 60 feet, and furnished to the ground with the most luxuriant growth. The bank of Rhododendrons and Azaleas were magnificent, and arranged in colour so as to produce the best effect while in flower. The broad gravel walks which wind through it are bordered by rich shrubberies, rare flowering plants and well kept short grass. The garden contains a good lawn tennis ground for recreation, and a cosy summerhouse to rest in and shun the heat, or to shelter from pelting showers. In an adjacent shady Pine plantation Mr Llewelyn showed us a collection of some of the new and more tender kinds of Rhododendrons that he is trying to inure to the climate of Penllergare. The plants were making strong healthy growths, and Mr Llewelyn is sanguine that many of them will prove hardy when planted in sheltered situations in the woods.

Again one is obliged to Mr Pettigrew for this description in *The Journal of Horticulture and Cottage Gardener* in 1886.

THEREZA DILLWYN LLEWELYN with a telescope. 1850s.
Collodion image by John Dillwyn Llewelyn.
Top: the full negative.
Bottom: as printed to pretend it was an interior scene.

THE UPPER LAKE, PENLLERGARE.
Mid-1850s. Collodion image by
John Dillwyn Llewelyn.

## A VICTORIAN PARADISE

Despite years of neglect, the core of the Penllergare estate is, today, still rich in plant, animal and bird life. Careful searching of the undergrowth may reveal a variety of wild flowers and all around are many of the original trees, now mature, that have survived from the time of John Dillwyn Llewelyn. Probably also many of the rhododendrons and azaleas that proliferate owe their origins to his plantings, or those of his son.

Whilst the more formal areas of the estate, such as the Observatory Garden and the Front Garden, have long vanished, the woodlands still show evidence of their careful planning and layout. In setting out the estate, with its pathways, streamlets and drives, John cleverly followed the natural contours of the land, and by so doing he gave his design a totally natural look.

John was much influenced in his botanical and natural history interests by his father Lewis Weston Dillwyn, a noted botanist. Dillwyn's earliest publication *The Botanists Guide through England and Wales,* written in association with his old school friend Dawson Turner,[33] was published in 1805. Unfortunately, he did not list any plants found at Penllergare in the version as published. But there is a copy of the publication, originally in two volumes, that has been rebound with blank pages between each printed page.[34] Inserted into the section on Glamorgan have been added a number of specimens found at Penllergare by various members of the family and friends, including some listed as discovered by Henry Talbot, and others, in the 1830s. Two such discoveries 'Conferva mirabilis, Penrice and Penllergare  Mr Dillwyn' and 'Bryum --- punctatum.  Woods at Penllergare  ld [WHFT]' may have been made when Talbot, Constance and the children came down to South Wales to stay with his relations in 1838.[35]

In Dillwyn's unpublished *Materials for a Flora and Fauna of Swansea and the Neighbourhood* written in 1848 specially for the visit and meeting of the British Association for the Advancement of Science, there are references to flora and fauna found around Penllergare. The hen harrier and the 'reed wren' were found in the woods, and siskins were abundant in the alder bushes. Nuthatches were also frequent visitors as was the goat sucker or night jar.

Lewis Weston Dillwyn's place in the sciences of botany and zoology, both nationally and locally, is secure.[36] He was elected a Fellow of the Royal and the Linnean Societies and amongst his many personal friends were the Hookers of Kew, Joseph Sabine,[37] former Secretary of the Horticultural Society, and Robert Brown, Librarian of the Linnean Society.[38] Other friends included Charles Babbage,[39] the inventor of the calculating machine, a forerunner of the computer, and Thomas Bowdler,[40] a resident of Oystermouth and famous for his expurgated editions of Shakespeare.

Dillwyn's relationship with the Hooker family was continued by his son John and in turn by his daughter Thereza Llewelyn. The archives of the Royal Botanic Gardens at Kew contain a number of letters from the family to the Hookers. One of the earliest references in the Diary of Lewis Weston Dillwyn for 21 March 1817 says 'Write to Hooker'. In 1839 William Jackson Hooker was the recipient of a copy of Dillwyn's latest publication *Hortus Malabaricus of Henry van Rheede van Draakenstein* published in Swansea. He also received a copy of the two last chapters of Dillwyn's *Contributions towards a History of Swansea* and in 1843 a copy of his *Hortus Collinsonianus*[41], an account of the plants cultivated by Peter Collinson FRS.

In April 1842 John accompanied his father on a visit to William Jackson Hooker. Dillwyn's Diary entry of Saturday 23 reads:

> John & I started about noon for Kew with Robt Brown. Went first to West Park, Sir W Hookers residence & afterwards found him at the Gardens where we remained nearly 3 hours. John on his return called at the Chiswick Horticultural Garden & at 7 we 3 met at the Athenaeum with de la Beche to dine. Afterwards went to Soirees at Murchisons[42] and Babbages.

The following day Dillwyn took his son to dine with Sir James South, the astronomer.

In 1848 Lewis Weston Dillwyn, in his role as President of the Royal Institution of South Wales of which he was also a founder, and in his capacity as a Vice President of the British Association for the Advancement of Science, welcomed the delegates to their conference in Swansea and wrote for them his short monograph on the local flora and fauna already referred to. One of the visitors was the botanist George Bentham who stayed with the Llewelyns at Penllergare. John, like his father, a member of the British Association for the Advancement of Science, was a Vice President of 'Section B - Chemical Science including its application for Agriculture and the Arts.'

What the estate looked like prior to the occupation of the Dillwyns in 1817 and John Dillwyn Llewelyn's great work is unknown. It was probably well-wooded but in a sorry state, and Lewis Weston Dillwyn recorded in his Diaries his efforts to tidy up and replant the woodlands. A few watercolours depict the old mansion prior to the work carried out by Haycock. But these show only the immediate surroundings of the house and nothing of the areas now containing the Lakes and Waterfall. In the auction catalogue of 1936 there are books that might have revealed these secrets, but any chances of finding them seems remote. Papers, not considered of any importance, were simply thrown away.[43]

John himself speculated on how things might have appeared, and one of the stories he wrote for his children about Oystermouth includes such a description. The hero of the story, young Walter Fitzherbert, is captured by the marauding Welsh and imprisoned in their camp which is at, where else, but Penllergare. The local chieftain is, however, a gentleman and tells Walter:

> This is my favourite spot, & for ages past this has been the chosen seat of British princes, and the head of the Welsh encampment, its name signifies this. It is called Penllergare and here my forces are now assembled.

Young Walter manages to escape following a drunken orgy by the warriors. He breaks out of his tent and quietly slips away:

> The camp was now behind him and the quiet depth of the valley with her rushing stream and solemn wood lay before ... The impetuous river with a hollow sound, murmured from the depth below, and the gentle wind fanned the tall trees ... He however waited but a moment, and then determining his course he hesitated no longer, but descended the steep side of the valley, and plunged into the thick masses of holly bushes, which made them an impervious evergreen covert.[44]

It was in 1839 that John began work on the three main features of the estate, the two Lakes and the Waterfall. Again, sadly, no original plans or bills for work carried out survive but there are some contemporary comments to be found in the *Cambrian*. The Upper Lake, also known as the Fish Pond, descends over a man-made Waterfall whence the water flows into the Lower Lake and then continues on downwards to Cadle. On 1 September 1839 the *Cambrian* reported that John Dillwyn Llewelyn had

> formed the Upper and Lower Lakes, which impound vast quantities of water, at about one-fortieth the cost of the public reservoirs which hold no larger quantity.

The Upper Lake is now less romantic and picturesque than it was in John's days when the view extended upwards to a wooden bridge, stone steps, moored boats and an old cottage. Here too could be seen the lovely little shanty made from old timbers with the front supported by an old tree. In the summer this was decorated with roses growing all over the roof and, when photographed, was called 'Fairy Land.' Somewhere also along the banks of the Upper Lake was the scene for a beautiful photograph called the 'Birchbark Canoe.' In the middle of the Lake can be seen small islands, once well covered with trees and doubtless the scene of many a fishing expedition after the local trout.

At the bottom end of the Upper Lake is the Waterfall. This triumph of Victorian engineering and materials is entirely man-made and retains the original sluices which were still in working order in the early 1990s. When the water levels are high and the stream running swiftly, it is a most magnificent sight with the main fall and smaller falls each side. The trees and general appearance make one believe that this spot has not changed at all since John made his many photographic images of the scene.

Downwards from the Waterfall is a modern bridge crossing the water, but below the modern structure you can still see the rounded supports of the Old Stone Bridge, a favourite feature of many of the old photographs. The water continues to rush downwards and eventually comes out in the Lower Lake, an area of almost twenty acres. At the entrance to the Lake stood the Boathouse.

The construction of the Lakes was carried out by unknown local men. What survives today is a memorial to their great work. A massive stone dam was built at the end of the Lower Lake with an intricate series of tunnels to prevent the Lake from flooding. There was also a sluice gate, removed when the Lower Lake was drained and a Lower Fall, also now gone.

On 23 August 1839 Mrs Mary Dillwyn had her first view of the Lakes having only recently returned with her husband Lewis Weston Dillwyn from a ramble in the Lake District. Dillwyn wrote:

> At about 10 to 10 we left Sketty Hall with our own Horses as far as Penllergare, and there Madame had never seen the new Lake since the water has been let in and we descended the Banks so as to enable us to compare it with its northern rivals.

One of the now vanished buildings on the estate was the Boathouse sited beside a stream running into the Lower Lake. As well as housing the boats used on the Lake it was also the scene for family picnics. For example on the eleventh birthday of the youngest daughter, Lucy, the family had their dinner in the Boathouse 'and fried bacon and eggs & fish for ourselves.'

Emma Llewelyn kept a notebook in which she recorded all kinds of household facts and details, and in its pages she listed all those items needed 'for a pic-nic in the Boat House' on the Lower Lake.

|  |  |
|---|---|
| Corkscrew | 3 Baskets |
| Wine | Matches |
| Beer | Faggot |

THE WATERFALL BETWEEN THE LAKES. *c*.1855. Collodion image by John Dillwyn Llewelyn.
Exhibit No.507 in the Photographic Society of London Exhibition 1856.

Top: THE BOATHOUSE ON THE LOWER LAKE. *c.*1852. Calotype by
John Dillwyn Llewelyn.
Bottom: BOAT ON THE LOWER LAKE. *c.*1852. Calotype by John Dillwyn Llewelyn.

Jug to fetch water                        Paper
Plates (small)
Dishes
Knives forks spoons
Glasses
Frying pan
Table cloth
Coarse cloths  2 or 3
Bread
Butter - little pot & plate
Eggs - a basin to <u>beat</u> <u>them</u> in for omelette
Bacon
Salt             )
Pepper        ) in a box
Parsley

Wildlife proliferated on the Lakes. Otters were established in the Lower Lake area, and in John's time it was quite permissible to hunt the animals. On 24 May 1845 Lewis Weston Dillwyn described an otter hunt:

> Drove with Mr Janson[45] to an Otter Hunt at Penllergare & we did not get back to Dinner till near 7 - An otter was found soon after 11 & then hunted without intermission was left uncaught at $\frac{1}{4}$ to 6. My side being troublesome I did not get into a Boat & only saw the sport from the close neighborhood of the Boat House on the Lower Lake.

John travelled to London to find suitable waterfowl for his Lakes and in an undated latter to his sister Fanny records 'added many beautiful ducks and geese to my collection.'

A few years after the death of John Dillwyn Llewelyn, when Andrew Pettigrew of Cardiff visited Penllergare he wrote a vivid account of the landscape. As he entered the estate from the lower end at Cadle, he looked downwards to the Lower Lake:

> The view from the left side of the road is hemmed in by the rock out of which it is cut, and the rising ground above it. Advantage has been taken of the narrowness of the valley here to make a lake by throwing a bank across it and damming the stream. The lake is beautifully situated and its surface along the margin is covered with different kinds of Water lilies, while the steep banks on all sides are wooded down to the water's edge. In the middle of the bank, at the lowest end of the lake, there is a strong bulwark composed of large blocks of stone, which forms the resisting power to the heavy weight of water at a point where the lake forms a cascade, which leaps boldly over a fall of 18 feet, and then the river assumes its natural course down the valley till it is interrupted, where it forms another lake of

greater dimensions. Both lakes are well stocked with trout, which afford good sport to Mr. Llewelyn and his friends from boats during the fishing season.

From this point the drive continues to rise gradually till it emerges in front of the mansion on a small open plateau, which is neatly laid out in shrubberies, flower beds and plots of well-kept short grass. Here the ground immediately to the right descends to the lake, and for some distance past the east side of the house. Shady winding walks lead from the mansion down to the lake, and along its side nearest the house, past the cascade, and down the right side of the stream for a great distance till it is crossed by a bridge, where the walks diverge into the woods and ascend the opposite bank. Osmunda regalis and other British ferns in great variety grow luxuriantly in every available spot, and fringe the banks and sides of the stream abundantly.

Mr Pettigrew went on to describe the immense number of rhododendrons, both species and hybrids, growing on the estate, and informed the reader that every year thousands of new seedlings were planted out. The descendants of these rhododendrons, seen by Mr Pettigrew, can still be found amongst the interloping *ponticums* (common rhododendrons) that proliferate today. One that has been recently discovered is *Pengaer*, a hybrid of *thomsonii* x *griffithianum*, that received an Award of Merit from the Royal Horticultural Society in 1911. Until this recent discovery it was believed to have been lost to cultivation.

Enthusiastic gardeners have always been keen to swap plants and information with each other and John was no exception. Though he bought at several of the well-known nurseries he also acquired plants from friends. As already mentioned his botanical friends included George Bentham, the Hookers of Kew, Lady Mary Cole and his wife's cousin Henry Talbot.

Henry Talbot, apart from his photographic interests, was also a keen horticulturalist. In a letter otherwise concerned with photography, Talbot wrote to John on 21 May 1852:

> I hope your garden prospers. I recommend you if you have not got it the Tacsonia manicata[46]. I never saw any climber that can be compared with it for beauty, hanging in festoons and covered with brilliant scarlet flowers, my plant will have borne this season many hundred flowers one being produced in the axil of every leaf and about 20 or 30 opening every day.

Who actually planned the Penllergare landscape is unknown. Probably it was John himself assisted by members of his family and possibly also influenced by Loddiges,[47] the Hackney horticulturists. George Loddiges was a friend of Lewis Weston Dillwyn and the Loddiges, along with Millers, Knights and Veitches, were sources of plants for the estate.

Mrs Mary Dillwyn herself was a keen gardener, as was Lady Mary Cole. Mrs Dillwyn consulted Lady Mary on such matters and wrote to her on 3 September 1832:

Do tell me soon you will repeat your visit - I want to consult you about many things - John is making a Flower Garden and wants to plan his new Road, all matters of Taste in which your advice would be most valuable & thankfully received - so pray come.

Someone, probably a member of the family, has left a remarkable drawing of the estate at this period. It is almost a bird's-eye view but shows very dramatically the complete layout, with the mansion dominating the horizon and looking down over the wooded landscape and the Lakes.

SKETCH FROM A LETTER. John Talbot Dillwyn Llewelyn to his mother. 6 November 1853.

PANORAMA OF PENLLERGARE. Artist unknown but the handwriting may be that of Thereza Dillwyn Llewelyn.
It shows the house and estate from the east flank of the Llan valley after the work carried out by Edward Haycock.

RHYNCHOSTYLIS RETUSA. Mid-1850s.
Photograph by
John Dillwyn Llewelyn.

## THE KITCHEN GARDEN & THE ORCHID HOUSE

The dual carriageway from Swansea via Fforestfach to the motorway covers the area that was the Home Farm and cuts off that part of the estate which originally extended towards the village, then known as Gorseinon and now called Penllergaer. The Home Farm included a large pond that supplied water to the Orchid House. Houses now stand on this edge of the estate and near the area formerly called the Kitchen Garden. Within the area of the Kitchen Garden is the Walled Garden and within this are the remains of the Orchid House.

Andrew Pettigrew wrote about this area in his article for the *Journal of Horticulture and Cottage Gardener* in 1886:

> The kitchen garden, which lies high and exposed to the north-east, contains five acres, the forcing and plant houses, melon ground, gardener's house, and bothy. The inner portion of the garden is enclosed by walls, and the outer portion by tall hedges and shrubberies for shelter. The ground is laid out in convenient quarters for cropping, which are divided by gravel walks. The borders on either side of the principal walks are planted with espalier and pyramidal fruit trees at suitable distances from the walk. The trees, however, do not grow freely nor bear fruit satisfactorily on account of the exposed situation of the garden. It is different with the trees on the walls, which grow vigorously and mature heavy crops of fruit in good seasons. There is a good Peach wall here with a projecting framework of glass under the coping, which affords protection to a fine lot of trees in the best of health, and at the time of my visit were laden with fruit the size of pigeons' eggs. The varieties consisted of Lord Palmerston, one of the best of the large late varieties which ripen in the end of September; Prince of Wales, another excellent

late variety, fruit tender, melting and juicy; Barrington, an old standard variety that should be grown in every collection; Early Alfred, which ripens in the beginning of August; Dr Hogg, an excellent variety ripening in August; and Hardwick Nectarine, which is one of the hardiest and most prolific in cultivation. The different quarters in the kitchen garden were cropped systematically, each being filled with vegetables of one kind, the dwarfer and choicer sorts by themselves, and the cooler and stronger-growing kinds were treated in like manner, a quarter being devoted to Rhubarb, Artichokes, Asparagus, Peas, etc. The smaller fruits - Gooseberries, Currants, Raspberries and Strawberries - were grown on the same principle.

The Melon ground is one of the best I have seen for some time. It is convenient to the forcing and plant houses, and is completely shut in and sheltered by high hedges. It contains a good many pits and frames for bedding and other plants, and plenty of open space for growing and plunging plants during the summer, and for storing hardy plants in winter. It is here that the seedling Rhododendrons, Azaleas, and coniferous plants are grown in boxes until they are sufficiently large to be bedded out in nursery lines. Mr Warmington had growing here an excellent assortment of Liliums in 11-inch pots, amongst which were L. Fortunei, L. speciosum, L. longiflorum bicolor, L. marmoratum, L. sanguineum, and others. They were growing in a compost of equal parts of peat and loam, which seemed to suit them admirably.

The whole area within the high stone walls is now scarcely recognisable from the above description. It is more an unruly collection of bracken and brambles, which at least serve to deter intruders! Here and there is a fern plant looking somewhat grander than its more lowly and prolific relations, and it must surely be a descendant of those which appear in several of John Dillwyn Llewelyn's photographs.

The Orchid House now stands forlorn, with its remaining walls playing host to sycamore trees and ivy, though the latter is probably doing a good job of holding the remaining structure together. However, the general outline is still discernible, the cistern is probably intact and much of the waterfall survives. This was probably one of the very first, if not the first, private purpose-built orchid houses in Britain. In *The Historic Gardens of Wales* published by Cadw in 1992 the author Elisabeth Whittle writes:

> Perhaps the saddest Welsh loss is the pioneering orchid house built in 1843 by John Dillwyn Llewelyn at Penllergare. It was an epiphyte house for non-terrestrial orchids. In it he attempted to create a tropical landscape, based on the Essequibo rapids, where one of the orchids he wanted to grow, *Huntleya violacea*, had been discovered. Above a central pool hot water splashed down in a series of rocky ledges, creating a hot, steamy atmosphere. The orchids flourished and visitors were amazed by their 'wild luxuriance'. Now all that remains is an untidy and overgrown jumble of stone. Thirty years later an orchid house was a standard element in the grander garden.

FUNGI FOUND NEAR THE OBSERVATORY.
28 September 1859. Watercolour by
Emma Charlotte Dillwyn Llewelyn.

GIANT HOGWEED IN THE QUARRY. 1864. Watercolour by Emma Charlotte Dillwyn Llewelyn.

INTERIOR OF THE ORCHID HOUSE. 1846. Watercolour by George Delamotte.

Left: ERIA DILLWYNII. Painted by W Fitch. Curtis's Botanical Magazine 1 June 1845.

Right: LELIA MAJALIS. From an original drawing by Emma Thomasina Dillwyn Llewelyn.

OSMUNDA REGALIS ON THE DRIVE.
Top: Hand-coloured photograph by John Dillwyn Llewelyn.
Bottom: Watercolour by Emma Charlotte Dillwyn Llewelyn.

In fact the origins of the building go back well before 1843. The year 1835 saw a great spending spree by John and amongst the many plants he purchased were orchids. The first reference to an actual building is in a letter dated 29 July 1836 to his father when he writes:

> The Stove has a great promise ... all know that.
> The back of the stove which I had left unfinished, in doubt whether to turn it into a common shed, or another stove, I have now determined on glazing - It will be only small and entirely given up to Orchis – 100 degrees of heat and an atmosphere saturated with water, is the enjoyment I promise myself and my pets - I intend them to flower there and to rest after the exertion in a dryer and cooler place.

A number of specimens from John's stove were used to illustrate articles in Curtis's *Botanical Magazine*, and probably the first time that photography was used to identify specimens was when John sent some daguerreotypes of his orchids to Sir John Hooker at Kew in 1842. Alas, these images no longer exist.

In 1846 an article written by John, and accompanied by illustrations, appeared in the first *Journal of the Horticultural Society*. Fortunately for us today, this article also included a ground plan and elevation of the building together with a drawing of the waterfall end.

John made use of several botanical explorers who travelled widely for specimens to bring back home. Already by 1833 he was in contact with Kew Gardens regarding an expedition to collect orchids.

On 15 October 1836 John wrote to William Jackson Hooker at Kew seeking further information regarding a proposed expedition to Brazil by George Gardener:

> At page 226 of the first volume of the companion to the Botanical Magazine, and again at the commencement of the second volume, I find a notice of an expedition to the Brazil mountains undertaken by Mr George Gardener[48] who proposes to offer collections of the flora of that country to those who may subscribe for them - Now though the terms for dried collections are there mentioned, the particulars of the subscription for seeds and plants are not specified, nor is the place or manner mentioned in which application for shares should be made, and I trust that my wish to procure this information will be sufficient excuse for this trespassing upon your time. It is orchideous plants, in which the district Mr Gardener proposes to explore is so rich, that I should be most anxious to procure, and as they can be transported with greater ease than most other plants I suppose that he contemplates sending home the living pseudo-bulbs for distribution.[49]

The inspiration for the actual design of his Orchid House came from the accounts written by Robert Schomburgk[50] of his visit to the Essequibo river in Guiana. As John Dillwyn Llewelyn wrote, in the first *Journal of the Horticultural Society*:

INTERIOR OF THE ORCHIDEOUS HOUSE AT PENLLERGARE.
Frontispiece from the *Journal of the Horticultural Society*, Volume 1 1846.

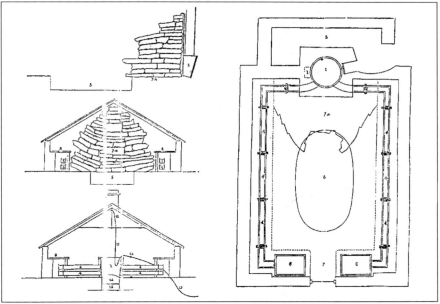

Top: INTERIOR OF THE ORCHID HOUSE. Mid-1850s. Photograph by John Dillwyn Llewelyn.
Bottom: PLAN OF THE ORCHID HOUSE. *Journal of the Horticultural Society* Volume 1 1846.
1 The Boiler & Flue. 2 The Fireplace. 3 Coalshed. 4 Hot-water pipes. 5 Water tank. 6 Hot-water cisterns.
7 Doorway. 7a Rockwork. 11 Pipe with hot water to fall over the rock-work. 12 Cold water pipe.
13 Stop-cock. 14 Boiler. 15 Ash-pit.

The account of the splendid vegetation which borders the cataracts of tropical rivers, as described by Schomburgk, gave me the first idea of trying this experiment. I read in the *"Sertum Orchidaceum"* his graphic description of the falls of the Berbice and Essequibo, on the occasion of his first discovery of *Huntleya violacea*.[51]

During his visit to Guiana, Schomburgk discovered a giant water lily six feet across which he named *Victoria Regina* in honour of Queen Victoria. In the spring of 1852, when he visited Hooker, John Dillwyn Llewelyn was promised a seedling.

It is also possible that some of the capability to install a system for heating the orchids by steam, came from Loddiges Nursery. George Loddiges had invented such a method and was the first commercial grower to put it into use.

Many rare and exotic plants were to be found growing at Penllergare. In the hot houses could be found bananas, pineapples and other tropical fruit and even tea, coffee and sugar. In 1835 John visited Knight's nursery gardens in London where he purchased orange trees and a tea tree. This caused him to write home with more than a touch of humour that 'I bought a green and black tea tree which as they only cost 2/6 each, I intend to put to good account - and close my dealing with Twining.'

Let us turn to Mr Pettigrew again for his description of the Walled Garden when he visited Penllergare in 1886:

> After leaving the Melon ground with its many objects of interest, we were shown through the forcing and plant house. The first of these, a lean-to greenhouse, was furnished with a good selection of Tuberous Begonias, Vallotas, Pelargoniums, and a choice of cool Orchids. The roof was partly covered by a large plant of Lapageria alba, which grows vigorously and flowers freely, the flowers lasting for a long time in perfection before fading. Next to this is an Orchid house, which contains a rich collection of well-grown plants, clean and healthy. Mr Llewelyn is a good orchidist, and perhaps it would not be too much to say that he inherits his love for them from his late father, who was deeply interested in their introduction and cultivation, that he and another gentleman employed a collector of Orchids between them long before Orchideæ became so common in this country. The following are a few of the varieties that were in favour or throwing up spikes at the time of my visit - Cypripedium barbatum, C. Lowi, C. iveum, C. caudaium, C. Pearcie, C. superbieus, C. Lawrencianum, C. Parishi, C. concolor, C. hirsutissimum, C. venustum, C. purpuratum, and C. Stonei. In close proximity to the latter was a large plant of Peristeria elata throwing up five spikes of great strength, and five large clumps of Dendrobium nobile in 14-inch pots, each pot having a little forest of pseudo-bulbs. Besides these there were fine pieces of D. Dalhousianum, D. Wardianum, D. macrophyllum, D. pulchelum, and others growing in boxes 2 feet square. There

were also good pieces of Aerides odoratum, A. crispum, and a large plant of A. odoratum purpurascens, with seventy spikes, Phalænopsis grandiflora, Vanda Cathcarti, Phaius maculatus, Dendrobium filiforma, Oncidium ampliatum with strong spikes 2 feet long. Besides these, there were large batches of Calanthus and other winter flowering varieties, some large plants of Eucharis strong and healthy, and a few specimen Pitcher Plants.

The next range consists of three lean-to vineries, each about 50 feet in length. The first of these was filled with a Black Hamburgh Vine some eighty years old. It is planted in an inside border and produces heavy crops of medium-sized bunches yearly. The second division is planted with Lady Downe's Seedling and Black Hamburgh, which were carrying heavy crops of large bunches. The third division is planted with late varieties which prolong the supply of Grapes to the end of March. The Vines in all the divisions were clean and healthy, and showed signs of good culture throughout.

When Sir John Talbot Dillwyn Llewelyn was in residence, it appears that he converted the Orchid House to propagate camellias. A brick wall was put around the central cistern and filled with earth and it was probably here that he planted the seedlings or cuttings. Today the only survivors of the camellias are the two fine specimens standing guard at the entrance to the remains of the building.

After the death of Sir John the estate fell gradually into decay. On 28 March 1928, the Walled Garden was rented as a nursery garden to, amongst others, Mr William Edge. Mr Edge ran a nursery garden there for twelve years until given twelve months notice to quit by the new tenants of Penllergare, the Welsh Bible College who, when they had raised sufficient money, proposed to purchase the mansion and gardens. This however never happened and the American army occupied the estate during the war. Seventy years after he took over the Walled Garden, Mr Edge was able to provide from memory a detailed plan of the original layout of the garden area, indicating the formal beds, pond and paths. There is also contemporary photographic evidence to show that both the Orchid House and the greenhouse against the wall survived until the arrival of the troops.

For many years the location of the Orchid House remained completely forgotten and it was a chance find by the then inhabitants of the Lower Lodge, in the 1980s, whilst wandering over the land near the dual carriageway from Fforestfach, which led them to contact the present author to find out if he could identify what they had discovered. At first, a few local people with knowledge of the estate denied that this could possibly be the site of the Orchid House which they placed within the Conservatory beside the mansion. However, production of the plans as illustrated in the *Horticultural Journal* for 1846, changed their minds. The author had long wished to discover the location of the Orchid House as it gave another insight into John's accomplishments beyond photography. That it is of major importance was confirmed by a number of experts in 1989/90. The then Curator, Royal Botanic Gardens, Kew, Mr J B E Simmons wrote:

The discovery of the footings from the Penllergare "Orchideous House" is obviously of considerable interest to garden historians. I believe this house marked a significant advance in the creation of landscaped interiors.[52]

Edward Diestelkamp of the National Trust wrote:

I was very interested to learn you think the remains of John Dillwyn-Llewelyn's conservatory [*sic*] still survive. I believe Dr Elliott of the Royal Horticultural Society is very well qualified to stress the importance of this conservatory, and the influence it had on nineteenth-century conservatories. The romantic "wild" interior influenced later conservatories and it was widely described and illustrated in horticultural journals throughout Europe.[53]

Carlton B Wood, a 1989-90 Martin McLaren Fellow, also referred to it as unique in his thesis for the Planning Unit, Royal Botanic Gardens, Kew. In a letter he wrote:

First and foremost, Mr Llewelyn's orchid house appears to be one of the earliest (if not the first) documented glasshouse display in Britain which attempted to recreate the naturalistic feel of a tropical landscape... Thirdly it appears that Mr Llewelyn was quite a knowledgeable man when it came to the culture of orchids. He was one of a handful of men who used nature as his guide when it came to creating environments in which orchids might flourish... The other important aspect of Mr Llewelyn's orchid house is the role it played in influencing other horticulturists. It was featured in the 1846 *Journal of Horticulture*, 1850 *Gardeners Chronicle and Agricultural Gazette* and the 1856 *Cottage Gardener and Country Gentleman's Companion*.

Dr Brent Elliott, Librarian and Archivist of the Royal Horticultural Society, also refers to the building in his book *Victorian Gardens*[54] quoting from the article in the *Journal of the Horticultural Society* 1846.

There can be no doubt from the evidence provided that this building is of great importance in the history of orchid growing and that John Dillwyn Llewelyn played a significant part in the development of orchid culture.

ROYAL INSTITUTION OF SOUTH WALES, SWANSEA. Engraving from the *Illustrated London News* based on a calotype by the Revd Calvert R Jones.

## *VISIT OF THE BRITISH ASSOCIATION FOR THE ADVANCEMENT OF SCIENCE*

n 1848 the Lower Lake was the scene of an event of great importance. Since 1841 John had been experimenting with building a boat powered by an electric motor, and the first reference is in his father's Diary for 6 January 1841:

> Drove in the afternoon to meet John at Lewis' Laboratory to try a small electric galvanic apparatus invented by Mr Hill for propelling Boats instead of Steam. It worked most beautifully and John is constructing a larger Machine for an experiment with his Boat on the Lake at Penllergare.

A further Diary entry for 9 January records that John was shown 'some beautiful experiments in galvanism' by Mr Hill. Details of Mr Hill's original motor were published by the London Electrical Society in 1841.

Benjamin Hill of Clydach, in the Swansea Valley, was one of the Committee planning the visit of the British Association for the Advancement of Science to Swansea in 1848. He was described in the *Annual Report of the Royal Institution of South Wales* for 1892-3 by the President, Samuel Gamwell, as an amiable eccentric whose father had come from the Midlands to work on the new canals.

The British Association meetings in Swansea allowed delegates time to visit local places of interest, and on Saturday 12 August they visited Penllergare together with the correspondents of the *Illustrated London News* and the *Cambrian* for a display of the electric boat on the

Upper Lake. Unfortunately, Michael Faraday, who was attending the meeting, was not present, but amongst those who did witness the display were Sir Charles Wheatstone and Sir William Grove.

The *Cambrian*, in their Supplement for 18 August, gave an eye-witness account of the visit to Penllergare and a description of the boat:

> ELECTRICITY A MOTIVE POWER FOR VESSELS:- One of the most interesting of the excursions was that to Penllergare, the mansion of J.D.Llewelyn, Esq., about five miles from Swansea. The mansion and grounds were not only liberally thrown open during that day, but a cold collation, with champagne and other wines, was provided by the hospitable owner, together with provender and accommodation for the horses of the visitors, who were numerous, including the Bishop of St David's, and many of the elite of the scientific professors, especially those interested in the science of electricity. Such was the demand indeed for carriages and horses that the available supply of Swansea would have been exhausted but for the liberal accommodation afforded by many private individuals... The favourable weather made the drive to and fro, and the promenade on the grounds and on the shores of the lake, truly delightful. The boat, which was impelled by the electric current, was, however, the principal object of attraction. It was not constructed for the purpose, but was the boat ordinarily used in the lake for pleasure purposes, capable of conveying about six persons, and the construction of which is due to J D Llewelyn, Esq., (the host of this scientific party), and our talented countryman Mr B Hill. A reference to a similar attempt made some years since in a far distant country (Russia), may not prove unacceptable to such of our readers as feel an interest in the history of scientific pursuits - in watching the successive steps by which men's minds progress in the cause of improvement.

The *Cambrian* account then described the earlier experiment that took place in Russia in 1838. The article concluded with a detailed description of the motive power used at Penllergare and ended by stating:

> The large body of visitors who witnessed the ingenious contrivance, expressed the greatest satisfaction at the result of the trial of electro-motive power.

From the description in the *Cambrian* it must be assumed that the boat at Penllergare was driven by propellers placed over the rear of the boat rather than through a shaft via the bottom of the boat. Unfortunately, Lewis Llewelyn Dillwyn, John's brother, did not attend this gathering as he was busy at the Pottery and we have no extant description of the experiment by any member of the family. Unfortunately also, the photographic process of the time, the Calotype, was not used to record the event. There can be no doubt, however, that this event was a most important occasion for the cause of science and also for South Wales.

LASTREA DILATATA AT PENLLERGARE. *c.*1855. Collodion image by John Dillwyn Llewelyn.
Probably Exhibit No.444 in the Photograhic Society of London Exhibition 1856.

STEPS AT THE END OF THE UPPER LAKE. Destroyed 'during making of railroad' *c.*1852.
Calotype by John Dillwyn Llewelyn.

THE OWLS OAK AT PENLLERGARE. 1850s. Collodion image by John Dillwyn Llewelyn.

THE LOWER FALL below the Lower Lake. *c.*1853. Calotype by John Dillwyn Llewelyn.

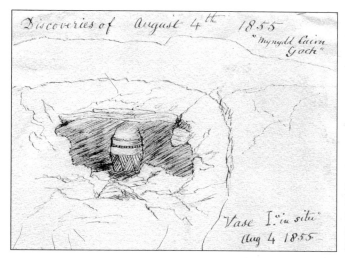

ANCIENT BRITISH VASES.
Discovered on Mynydd Carn
Goch by John Talbot Dillwyn
Llewelyn. He may also have
been the artist.

## *OTHER ACTIVITIES AT PENLLERGARE*

From a high vantage point on the estate one can see Llangyfelach church, formerly the Dillwyns' local church, in the far distance. The land between Llangyfelach and what is now the motorway was once also a part of the Penllergare estate and the site of some archaeological activities. In 1857 John Talbot Dillwyn Llewelyn discovered a cache of 'Ancient British' pottery on Mynydd Carn Goch. His father took the opportunity to make a photograph of these, and the ceramics themselves are now in the British Museum.

The Goppa, located on the hills above Penllergare, was a favourite site for picnics and in September 1855 John took his camera with him. The photograph was taken for Emma as a birthday present, something that John often did in the 1850s. A careful examination of the resulting image shows not only the various implements taken for such an event, but also a pigeon in the foreground. But is it alive? John made many photographs of birds and animals in natural places but the specimens were usually well and truly dead and often very moth-eaten as well.

In the late 1850s the scare of a French invasion led to the raising of Volunteer forces around Britain. In South Wales the 1st Corps was formed at Margam in 1859 under the command of CRM Talbot. The 3rd Corps was under the command of Lewis Llewelyn Dillwyn, and the 5th was formed at Penllergare on 12 October 1859 under John Dillwyn Llewelyn. John's Corps eventually merged with Lewis's 3rd. It was last listed and probably disbanded in 1873.

One of the duties of the commanding officer's wife was to provide the food for the meetings and social events which included shooting competitions. Emma Llewelyn has left accounts of these events in her little housekeeping notebook:

The Volunteer Summer feast, 1866, was mismanaged - there should have been, a donkey cart to convey the coffee & buns to the Rifle shed - Beer from Swansea - for the dinner - and directions for the Waiters at table - The Numbers present should always be ascertained, as a guide for the next time.

Oct 17 1866. Inspection of the Battalion - at Swansea
Breakfast at 11 - here - 323 men

| | | |
|---|---|---|
| 65 Buns | ) | |
| 20lb flour | ) | 20 of these, were carried down to |
| 1¾lb butter    salt | ) | Cadle for the Mynyddbach y Glo |
| 4lb currants | ) | contingent |
| 3lb sugar | ) | |
| a little spice | ) | |
| | | |
| 3¼lb coffee | ) | 60 were inspected in a field & all |
| 3½lb sugar | ) | went off well. Dinner in Music Hall |
| 7pts milk | ) | |

Oct 5 1867. Inspection at Penllergare. Volunteers 70 & 7 extra hands.

Shooting practice often took place at Penllergare and one of these events was recorded as a watercolour by young Emma Charlotte Llewelyn in 1860.

One event that did not actually take place at Penllergare, but is important in understanding the diversity of John's interests, was the visit of Charles Wheatstone in 1844.[55] Apart from references in the Diaries of Lewis Weston Dillwyn and Lewis Llewelyn Dillwyn, the event was not recorded by Wheatstone himself. In August 1844 Wheatstone, accompanied and assisted by John Dillwyn Llewelyn in a boat, conducted some sub-marine telegraphy experiments off Mumbles Head and demonstrated an electric bell between the lodge and house at Sketty.

The Penllergare estate, friends and family feature regularly in John's photographic activities. With a such a diversity of plant and wildlife available to him,  with frequent visits by local and more distant friends and relations, what more could he ask than to make them the subjects for his camera. But it is also worthy of note that his photographic activities stimulated other members of his family to take up drawing and painting activities as well. Thus, in a number of cases, we can see not only the exactitude of reproduction from the camera lens, but the actual colours of the more traditional artists' renderings. A later writer would claim that John Dillwyn Llewelyn was, in fact, a pre-Raphaelite photographer.[56]

OUR STAGE IN THE MORNING ROOM – PENLLERGARE. Sketch probably by Thereza Dillwyn
Llewelyn, as the caption is in her writing.

THE HYTHE VOLUNTEERS. 1859. John Dillwyn Llewelyn is wearing the top hat.
Photographer unknown.

WILLY LLEWELYN FISHING AT PENLLERGARE. 1855.
Collodion image by John Dillwyn Llewelyn.

THE RIVER AT PENLLERGARE. Mid-1850s. Collodion image by John Dillwyn Llewelyn.

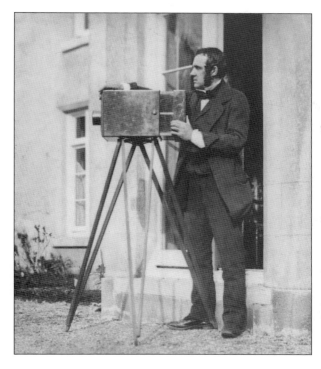

JOHN DILLWYN LLEWELYN 1853
with his calotype camera outside
Penllergare. Collodion image.
Possibly a self portrait.

## JOHN DILLWYN LLEWELYN – THE PHOTOGRAPHER

John Dillwyn Llewelyn's most important claim to fame undoubtedly lies in his pioneering contributions to the development of photography, though this in no way reduces his importance in other activities. It is interesting to realise that several of the early pioneers of photography were either Welsh or had strong links with Wales. The best known was the Revd Calvert Richard Jones, the third of the same name to live in Swansea. Jones was a close friend of John and their families were distantly related. And Henry Talbot, the father of photography, had strong Welsh family connections through his Welsh Talbot cousins at Penrice.

William Henry Fox Talbot (1800-77) was the only son of William Davenport Talbot of Lacock Abbey in Wiltshire and Lady Elisabeth Fox-Strangways, eldest daughter of the Earl and Countess of Ilchester. Elisabeth's younger sister, Lady Mary Theresa, married as her first husband Thomas Mansel Talbot (1747-1813) of Penrice and Margam, a cousin of William Davenport Talbot. Both the male Talbots had a common ancestor in John Ivory Talbot of Lacock Abbey who had married Mary, daughter of Thomas, 1st Lord Mansel of Margam.

A son, Christopher Rice Mansel, otherwise known as Kit, and seven daughters were born to Lady Mary and Thomas Mansel Talbot, including the youngest child Emma Thomasina, wife of John Dillwyn Llewelyn. Though his visits to South Wales were rare, their cousin Henry Talbot kept in contact through the years by correspondence.

From the very first days when photography was announced by Daguerre in France and Henry Talbot in England, John Dillwyn Llewelyn was an active and enthusiastic 'worker'. The contribution of Emma must also be acknowledged as she actively supported her husband and made many of his prints.

Until he was forced to make an announcement in 1839 owing to the rumours of a rival process from France, Talbot had remained secretive about his discovery and few, apart from his immediate family, were aware of his work. His cousins in Wales were not within this small group and it was not until 1838 that Emma's mother, Lady Mary Cole, was shown some of his work. She had been on a visit to Lacock Abbey to see her sister Elisabeth and on 28 February 1838, recording that visit in her Diary, wrote that 'Lily showed me many prints.' It was almost another year before Talbot would be forced to announce his discovery at the Royal Institution through Michael Faraday on 25 January 1839. Soon afterwards Henry Talbot sent his Aunt Mary a copy of the *Literary Gazette* of 2 February which included the first public announcement. Mary responded to her nephew on 9 February and wrote:

> Many thanks for your Literary Gazette. I am glad you showed me the little drawing while I was at Lacock because I comprehended it better than I otherwise should have done.

Henry Talbot also sent an example of his new photogenic drawing, as he called the process, to his cousin, Charlotte Traherne, who was staying with her husband at Penllergare at the time. She wrote to Henry on 28 February thanking him for the example of a photogenic drawing of a piece of lace. She continued:

> John Llewelyn has been making some paper according to your process and they have all been trying little scraps of lace and ribbon. One succeeded very well this morning before breakfast ... Mr Calvert Jones is quite wild about it and I dare say by this time is making experiments in Swansea himself.

Unfortunately, none of these very early examples have survived, but these and other letters show that the first early photographic experiments in Wales were conducted by John Dillwyn Llewelyn and at Penllergare. John was indeed 'smitten', and as well as trying Talbot's new process he also used that of Daguerre. Using the Daguerreotype process, which made an image on a piece of silver-plated copper, John made a picture of the Waterfall *c.*1843 and also one of the valley looking up towards the mansion. Members of the family were also popular subjects as was the Maypole at Penllergare, sometime in the early 1840s.

By September 1840 Henry Talbot had refined his process with the discovery that he could develop a latent image, thereby reducing exposure times and making it possible to take portraits.

THE OLD STONE BRIDGE below the Upper Falls.
Top: Collodion image, mid-1850s, by John Dillwyn Llewelyn
Bottom: Watercolour, 1864, by Emma Charlotte Dillwyn Llewelyn.

THE LOWER LAKE FROM NYDFWCH
Top: Collodion image, mid-1850s, by John Dillwyn Llewelyn.
Bottom: Watercolour, 1864, by Emma Charlotte Dillwyn Llewelyn.

JOHN DILLWYN LLEWELYN with his wet collodion apparatus. Mid-1850s. Many of the photographs at Penllergare were taken with this camera. Possibly a self portrait but, no doubt, with some assistance.

THE BIRCHBARK CANOE – A CANADIAN SCENE AT PENLLERGARE. Willy Llewelyn mending his fishing nets. c.1855. Collodion image by John Dillwyn Llewelyn. Probably Exhibit No.518 at the Photographic Society of London's Exhibition 1856.

He did not publicise the details until he took out a patent in 1843. Just when John Dillwyn Llewelyn first tried this new process is unrecorded. In a letter of 4 October 1841 Lady Mary Talbot wrote thanking her nephew Henry Talbot for the 'very handsome present of calotypes.' On 12 January the following year Henry Talbot's wife, Constance, was probably staying with, or had just left, his eldest cousin Mary Theresa Talbot. Constance wrote that day to say that she had given Mary some of the calotypes which she, in turn wanted

> for Mr Llewelyn who takes a great interest and wants to learn. He already has the Daguerreotype but I suppose is disgusted with its clumsiness and want of veracity, turning right things left etc.

Using the Calotype process John was able to make a great many images of Penllergare which are not only very beautiful as pictures but also reveal much about the estate. It is possible to identify groups of plants by the lake sides or even the type of stones used on the pathways. Some of his images are amongst the earliest examples of botanical photography, an area in which John excelled.

In 1851, a new process called the Wet Collodion process was announced by Henry Scott Archer. This process made negatives on glass rather than on paper and was also able to make far more rapid exposures. For example, the fastest recorded exposure by Talbot's Calotype process was one second. The new process could, under the right conditions, make exposures in a fraction of a second. This allowed John to make images of the waves in motion and active family events such as bonfire night in November. One of his earliest instantaneous images is of the waves in Caswell Bay dated 1853. In a letter to Peter Wickens Fry, a fellow photographer and visitor to Penllergare, John wrote:

> I have delayed sending until I (or rather Mrs Ll) had printed copies of 2 or 3 of my newer photographs - which I hope you may approve of.
> The weather just now in the country is dark and stormy, and I am not able to do much Camera work - but I am looking forward ere long to a campaign on the sea coast - for this I am making experiments daily and providing all the advantages that I can procure, both chemical and optical and manipulatory for the purpose of attacking the "restless waves" - all that I have hitherto done in this line convinces me that splendid pictures may be obtained under favorable circumstances, and I shall not spare trouble to secure such. I have some thought if I succeed as well as I hope, to exhibit at Paris. English photographers ought to be represented in France. Perhaps you can tell me what is doing in that way - are you or any of your friends proposing to send? [57]

To operate the Collodion process the photographer had to carry a great deal of equipment around with him which could weigh about a hundred pounds. The glass plates had to be prepared almost immediately before use and developed as rapidly as possible afterwards. For travellers this was a great problem and John set out to try and overcome the difficulty. In 1856 he was able to announce his new discovery, the Oxymel process, whereby the photographic plates having received an additional coating of oxymel, honey and vinegar to the collodion, could be preserved for some days. In some cases they were recorded as being perfect for use even after many weeks. *The Illustrated London News* for July 1856 rated this discovery as of extreme importance and benefit to photographers and especially tourists.

John's daughter Thereza was an equally ardent photographer and many of her images of Penllergare also survive. Especially interesting are her early stereoscopic views, as these give a three-dimensional effect when looked at with a special viewer. Her father gave her a new stereoscopic camera for her birthday in 1856 and she recorded that on June 13 she made an image of a stuffed hawk, and on June 21 John himself used the camera to make two images. Thereza also made some stereo images of scenes which her father took on his larger cameras.

Emma, though probably not taking any actual camera images herself, was John's hard-working printer. In these early days before the spread of the railway system, Emma would carry her own chemicals around in the family carriages, to make prints from her husband's negatives. So hard indeed did she work that Henry Talbot offered her the help of his own assistant, Nicholas Henneman, but she declined the offer.

Outside Penllergare and South Wales, John's photographic journeys were somewhat limited. He took some calotypes of Scottish scenes *c.*1852 and the family also made a number of visits to Cornwall, Bristol and Tenby, all occasions for energetic photographic activity. A visit to Yorkshire in 1856 also produced a series of excellent images. Sadly, John did not take his camera to mainland Europe on his various trips, preferring to rely on the purchase of local images and the watercolours produced by his daughters.

Others also photographed at Penllergare. These included James Knight, the tutor to the Llewelyn children, who has left images not only of Penllergare but also of Bristol when he and the Llewelyns visited that city in the 1850s. Philip Delamotte, nephew of George Delamotte who had made sketches of John and his family, and Hugh Owen, both known for their images of the Crystal Palace Exhibition, also took photographs on their visits to Penllergare. Antoine Claudet, one of the first daguerreotypists to operate professionally in London, and Peter Wickens Fry, a founder member of the Photographic Society of London, also visited Penllergare and the latter took some portraits of the family as well as some early images of Craig y Nos, later to become the home of Adelina Patti, the famous soprano.

In 1853 a group of photographers held a meeting at the Society of Arts, in London, and formed the Photographic Society of London, now the Royal Photographic Society. John was present at the meeting and became a member of the very first Council and remained a member of the Society for some years. The first President of the Society was Sir Charles Eastlake, President of the Royal Academy. John's fellow councillors included Charles Wheatstone, the Revd Calvert Jones of Swansea, Nevil Story Maskelyne who later married Thereza Llewelyn, Hugh Owen, and Peter Wickens Fry. At the Council Meeting on

PALMISTRY or GYPSIES. 7 September 1856.
Top: Stereo image by Thereza Dillwyn Llewelyn. Because the camera had only one lens, there was a delay before the second image could be take whilst the lens was moved across. Note how the smoke is different in both images.
Bottom: Collodion image by John Dillwyn Llewelyn. Group includes Johnny, Willy in the tent, Charlotte Traherne, Emma Charlotte with back to camera.

PIC-NIC ON GOPPA. September 1855. Collodion image taken for Emma's birthday by John Dillwyn Llewelyn.

REMEMBER, REMEMBER THE 5TH OF NOVEMBER. 1853. Collodion image by John Dillwyn Llewelyn. Queen Victoria so admired this image that she took a copy away from the Photographic Society of London's Exhibition in 1855. Members of the family with James Knight, both tutor and a photographer, on the left of the main group. This reproduction, from the original damaged negative, shows Emma Llewelyn on the far right. None of the prints made by John Dillwyn Llewelyn include her as it upsets the tight composition.

21 December 1854 it was 'resolved that Mr Llewelyn be nominated as the Country Vice-president...' though whether this resolution was ever ratified is not recorded.

John exhibited at all the Society's exhibitions from the very first in 1854 until 1858, receiving much praise for his work. Many of the photographs that he exhibited were either scenes of Penllergare or of the locality. In 1855 he was one of a British contingent that took part in the Exposition Universelle in Paris. For this he exhibited four images under the title of 'Motion'. One of them showed 'Waves breaking in Three Cliffs Bay' though anyone who knows the location will recognise it as under Shire Cwm in Pobbles Bay. Another showed a sailing ship off Caswell, the third was the steamer *Juno* blowing off steam at Tenby and the fourth captured a 'cloud over St Catherine's, Tenby.' For these John was awarded a silver medal. At the Society's exhibition in 1856 amongst his images exhibited was 'Remember, Remember the Fifth of November' showing his family around the Guy Fawkes bonfire. Thereza recalled in later years how Queen Victoria so admired the image that she carried it off with her and a new print had to be rushed from Penllergare. Prince Albert was at this time compiling his own collection of photographs, and his secretary Dr Becker, one of the original Council members of the Photographic Society of London, approached John for some of his images including a view of Caswell Bay. These photographs are still in the Royal Family's collection at Windsor Castle and appear in several albums including one which contained Queen Victoria's favourite images.

John's asthma probably prevented him from being photographically active beyond the late 1850s, but his interest in the art remained. He became, in the 1870s, a Member of the Amateur Photographic Association whose members included the Prince of Wales, and was on its Council.

One of the great advantages of photographs over the painted image is the 'reality recorded' though it was not impossible, even in the early days of photography, to alter the image on the negative. Details, not necessarily considered important by the painter, are often visible in the photograph. Photography though, in the earliest days, was unable to reproduce colour and it is the combination of the photographs by John with the watercolours by members of his family, that will provide such an important source for the future restoration of Penllergare.

After his death in 1882 many of John Dillwyn Llewelyn's achievements appeared to have been forgotten and even his son Sir John, in his later years, was unaware of the diversity of his father's accomplishments. His photographic negatives may have been given to his daughter Thereza, for her handwriting appears on many of the boxes now in the National Museums and Galleries of Wales. Few examples of his work were in public collections and it was not until 1977 that the first modern exhibition of his photographic images was held, at the Fox Talbot Museum at Lacock. Today, John Dillwyn Llewelyn is firmly established in his rightful place in the history of photography. His images are in many national collections including those of the Glynn Vivian Gallery in Swansea and the National Museums and Galleries of Wales in Cardiff. He even has the honour of having his name on the Internet, and for someone who knew Charles Babbage, the father of the computer, he would surely have been delighted.

71

COLLODION BRIDGE – PENLLERGARE. 1856. Collodion image by John Dillwyn Llewelyn.
'October 7 1856… we had a long walk with Papa, to the lower lodge, and home by the Valley, where we saw abundant traces of last night's flood, for the path by the watercressery was all torn up, debris thrown <u>over</u> the grass and path, and Bridges – whilst Collodion bridge was destroyed. The rain last night amounted to 1.54 – $\frac{1}{2}$ inch more that I ever remember before.' Journal of Thereza Dillwyn Llewelyn.

MRS DILLWYN AND THEREZA AT
PENLLERGARE. 1850s. Collodion image by
John Dillwyn Llewelyn.

## *ENVOI*

I n this brief account of the history of Penllergare and of John Dillwyn Llewelyn, it will be
very apparent how important a place he occupied in nineteenth-century history, especially
that of the Swansea area. His contributions to photography are now fully recognised. His
horticultural and botanical activities are now being seen in their true light and he is also
recognised as a pioneer in the cultivation of orchids.

But John is not the only member of his family to have contributed to Swansea's history. As
has already been noted, his father, Lewis Weston Dillwyn, gave fame to Swansea, first
through his management of the Swansea Pottery, through hosting the British Association for
the Advancement of Science in 1848 and through his botanical, zoological and political
activities. The Royal Institution of South Wales stands as his memorial both as one of the
founders and its first President. John's brother, Lewis Llewelyn Dillwyn, also a Mayor of
Swansea and on many of the local committees concerned with the town, was for many
years a Member of Parliament and Director of the Great Western Railway until his death in
1892. In addition, he owned a Spelter Works. Lewis's daughter Amy Dillwyn, who died in
1935, is still recalled by many, and the Amy Dillwyn Society is named after her. Amy's
distinctions included being Britain's first woman industrialist, running her father's Works
after his death and restoring it to profitability. She was also an author of some repute and a
part-time literary critic for the *Spectator*. In Swansea there are streets named after the
family and the Dillwyn Building Society only recently changed its name. Such, today, is the

recognised fame of the family that Lewis Weston Dillwyn, his sons John and Lewis and niece Amy are all included in the new *Dictionary of National Biography.*

Penllergare lies on Swansea's doorstep and within easy access of the motorway. For the people of Swansea, and its many visitors, here is a place where they might relax and enjoy nature without the noise of traffic and the hustle and bustle of daily life. Penllergare provides the opportunity to walk through the woods, listen to the birds and, maybe, even spot the wildlife in the Lower Lake or trout in the stream. Here, too, is the chance to discover the scenes captured in the old photographs and to imagine that John and Emma and the children are busy bustling about and setting up the scenes ready for their instant capture on paper or glass.

Swansea is fortunate to have such history on its doorstep and hopefully it will be made available for all to experience. So much of Penllergare's nineteenth-century glory has vanished. What is left must be preserved for future generations to enjoy before it is too late.


Richard Morris
1999

# THE PLIGHT AND POTENTIAL OF PENLLERGARE TODAY

L lewelyn's landscape has been described as one of the finest late Picturesque designs in Wales. According to Andrew Sclater in his seminal report on the Penllergare landscape, it is essentially simple, yet highly sophisticated and integrated, the layout exploiting the dramatic quality of its site of great natural beauty in a manner almost unrivalled in South Wales. 'It is a secret and magical place'.[58]

Now there is a car-park and municipal buildings where the mansion once stood. The M4 motorway has sliced off the top of the designed landscape and another dual carriageway shaves the western and southern boundaries. A substantial housing estate is beginning to encroach on the parkland and the far side of the valley is blocked by urban and industrial development. What remains inside this perimeter has suffered sustained dereliction and vandalism.

Against all the odds, however, much of the structure, and even some of the planting, still survive. Parts of the Drive, the Upper Lake and some of the paths have been roughly restored, as a condition of planning consent for the housing. The Waterfall is still relatively unscathed. Other structures, such as the remnants of the Walled Gardens (and the Orchideous House within) survive by default, owing their continued, precarious survival as much to swamping vegetation as to any efforts by man. Much more would be discovered through surveys and further study of the documentation and imagery because '... no other Welsh landscape, and probably very few in the world, has such an extensive archive of photography of outstanding quality'.

Neglect and comparative inaccessibility can often benefit wildlife and this is true of Penllergare, helped here, fortuitously, by the dam of the Lower Lake having been breached long since.[59] And in the valley, despite its proximity to the city centre and being surrounded by development, there is a sense there of wilderness, probably unique in South Wales.

When a comprehensive development scheme was being planned in the early 1990s, the idea of using the derelict remains of Llewelyn's private paradise for a country park was both enlightened and pragmatic. In the event, although many of the commercial benefits of the scheme were realised, there was a consistent and woeful failure either to protect the now-designated Grade II estate,[60] or to provide the promised recreational facilities.

Accordingly, the Welsh Historic Gardens Trust (initially) and now the Penllergare Trust, have recommended a fresh start and concerted action to restore the cultural landscape of Penllergare and to manage it as a public park of the highest quality. Otherwise its long-term future will continue to be bleak indeed.

Michael Norman
May 2002

CLICHÉ VERRE. 1840s. Drawn by a member of the family. This was made by coating a piece of glass with black lacquer, creating an image with a sharp pointed tool, and then printing the result onto photographic printing paper.

# NOTES AND COMMENTS

ATTENTION AND INATTENTION. 1840s. Watercolours from a story by John Dillwyn Llewelyn for his children, showing scenes at Penllergare.

[1] A word about the spelling of Penllergare. The house and estate have always been spelt Penllergare and the Estate Office to this day uses this spelling. It is therefore the form used throughout this publication. The village, now known as Penllergaer, was formerly called Gorseinon. Historically therefore the spelling of Penllergaer Park is incorrect!

[2] Edward Haycock, a Shrewsbury architect. He also designed Clytha Park in Monmouthshire and Holy Cross Church at Taibach, Port Talbot, was supervisory architect for Margam house, built by C R M Talbot and worked on Sketty Hall and Burrows Lodge for L W Dillwyn. He is also said to have been involved with Coedriglan, the home of the Revd J M Traherne, though popular belief is that Traherne designed the house himself.

[3] Unfortunately no photographs seem to exist of this area.

[4] The second son, John Crook Dillwyn, 1780-1 only appears in written documents which I have recently seen. It is also interesting that George Dillwyn, the younger surviving brother of Lewis, is not referred to in some family trees. He offended his Quaker relations with his liaison with the governess, Miss Gowing, whom he eventually married.

[5] St Mary's is the collegiate church of the University. Unfortunately they have no written records of the location of gravestones and many of those outside have disappeared. However, there is, on the floor inside, a small stone with several Adamses named on it including a Sarah. Further investigations in Oxford have produced no further details.

[6] *Casgliad o Waith Ieuan Deulwyn*, Ifor Williams, (Bangor 1909); privately printed for The Bangor Welsh Manuscripts Society.

[7] Painted at the behest of Lewis Weston Dillwyn. C R Leslie was a friend of the Dillwyns and also painted William Dillwyn, Lewis Weston, Mary Dillwyn and John. The latter paintings are still in the family whilst that of William is in the Friends Meeting House, Euston Road, London.

[8] Henry Hey Knight (1795-1857) cleric and antiquary. Revd William Bruce Knight (1785-1845), appointed Dean of Llandaff 1843.

[9] Henry Moule of Melksham, who was recommended by the Revd Francis Kilvert. The latter, uncle of the famous diarist, ran a school at Claverton, Bristol.

[10] Though he was christened William Henry Fox, Talbot hated the name William and never used it. Letters to his family are signed Henry or HFT. Early letters may also be signed WHFT. For example, in his letters from Harrow to his cousin Jane Harriot Talbot, though she is addressed as My dear Jane, they are signed WHFT. In the Diaries of Lewis Weston Dillwyn he is referred to as Henry Talbot, and Emma Llewelyn referred to him as Henry. Fox appears never to have been used by his intimates: it is a modern usage.

[11] Her name is usually spelled Theresa in early diaries and letters but her descendants prefer Thereza, which spelling she used herself.

[12] See *Oxford Rebels*, Vanda Morton (Alan Sutton, Gloucester, 1987) for an account of Maskelyne.

[13] Sir William Jackson Hooker (1785-1865). Born in Norwich. Married Maria, daughter of Dawson Turner FRS. Fellow of the Linnean Society 1806. Fellow of the Royal Society 1812. In 1836 he was made a Knight of Hanover for botanical services. First Director of the Kew Botanic Gardens, where with the Revd J S Henslow, Professor of Botany at Cambridge, he founded a museum of economic botany. He was succeeded as Director of Kew by his son Joseph Dalton Hooker (1817-1911).

[14] George Bentham (1800-84). Botanist. Second son of Sir Samuel Bentham and nephew of Jeremy Bentham. Born at Stoke, near Plymouth. His Herbarium arrived from France 1828. Elected to the Linnean Society 1828. His association with the Horticultural Society began in 1829 and he was Hon.Sec. until 1840. Presented his collection to Kew Gardens 1854. FRS 1862.

[15] See *Basset Down, an old country house*, Mary Arnold-Forster, a daughter of Thereza, (Country Life Ltd, undated).

[16] When asked what was the best time to live in, he replied 'Before the income tax'. Quoted in a private family book of party games and questions.

[17] This comment refers to John's two youngest children Elinor and Lucy.

[18] University of Wales, Swansea, Library, Folder A5.

[19] Burrows Lodge stood just behind the site of the Swansea Museum. In 1831 Lewis Weston Dillwyn purchased Sketty Hall, but extensive building work and improvements delayed the family's move into their new property until 1834. Lewis and Mary Dillwyn lived at Sketty Hall until their deaths. Mrs Llewelyn, widow of the Colonel, died at Burrows Lodge in 1831, and Mary de la Beche Dillwyn, elder daughter of Lewis Llewelyn Dillwyn, was born there in 1839. Lewis Llewelyn Dillwyn occupied Burrows Lodge prior to moving into Parkwern and building Hendrefoilan. The Moggridges resided at Burrows Lodge for a while. It appears to have been a short term residence for various members of the Dillwyn family but the security of which belonged to John after his father's death.

[20] *Contributions towards a History of Swansea* Lewis Weston Dillwyn. (Murray and Rees , Swansea 1840) Limited edition of 300 copies. Author's collection.

[21] Thomas Lloyd provided the author with this information and based his belief on the round staircase and other features which were typical of Jernegan. There are also similarities to another house, Stouthall, in Gower, which is known to be by Jernegan who also made designs for a number of buildings in Swansea.

[22] Benjamin Heath Malkin (1769-1842). Miscellaneous writer. Son of Thomas Malkin of St Mary-le-Bow, London. Educated Harrow and Trinity College, Cambridge. BA 1792. MA 1802. Headmaster of Grammar School, Bury St Edmunds. Fellow of the Antiquarian Society. Died Cowbridge, Glamorgan, 26 May 1842. His *Account of a new Tour of Wales* appeared in Pinkerton's General Collection of Voyages, 1808.

[23] Charles Robert Leslie (1794-1859). Painter. American born of Scottish parents. He was a friend of the Dillwyn family and made several portraits and sketches of them. His painting of *The Death of Sarah* hangs in the RISW (now the Swansea Museum).

[24] National Library of Wales, Penllergare archives B1-7.

[25] *Great Landowners of Britain*, John Bateman FRGS, (Harrison & Sons, London 1878).

[26] The Diaries of Lewis Weston Dillwyn are usually at the National Library of Wales on loan. They are currently back with the family and are being transcribed, hopefully to make them more readily available. Calendars of the Diaries were made in the 1930s by the National Library of Wales but omit many of the parts of the text then considered embarrassing to the descendants of those referred to in the originals.

[27] Sir James South (1785-1867). Astronomer. Born Southwark, eldest son of James South, dispensing chemist. Married  Charlotte Ellis of South Lambeth 1816. A co-founder of the

(Royal) Astronomical Society and President 1829. Knighted 1830.

[28] A reference to the great telescope at Birr Castle, Ireland, built by William, 3rd Earl of Rosse (1800-67) and recently restored. Rosse was one of those who played an important part in persuading Fox Talbot to relinquish his patent rights on the calotype process. His wife Mary was an early photographer. See *Impressions of an Irish Countess*, David H Davison, (The Birr Scientific Heritage Foundation, 1989)

[29] Thereza's Journals are in private family archives and are not published.

[30] David Mandre was probably a gardener on the Penllergare staff. He appears with a wheel barrow in one of John Dillwyn Llewelyn's photographs.

[31] Quoted in *Amy Dillwyn*, David Painting, (University of Wales Press, Cardiff, 1987) Original letters now on loan from the family to University of Wales, Swansea, Library. Harry was her elder brother.

[32] Copy of his letter was sent to the author.

[33] Dawson Turner (1775-1858). Botanist and antiquarian. Son of James Turner (1734-94) head of the Yarmouth Bank. Published many books. Co-author with L W Dillwyn of the *Botanists Guide*. Eldest daughter Maria married W J Hooker.

[34] National Library of Wales, Mss 14936-8B. I believe that this copy once belonged to Lewis Weston Dillwyn as the additional writing is in his hand.

[35] See Diary of Lady Mary Cole for that year. The Diary is now in the Fox Talbot Museum, Lacock.

[36] A brief account of his botanical and zoological interests appears in the *South Wales and Monmouth Record Society Publication No 5*, 1963, which also contains brief extracts from his Diaries.

[37] Joseph Sabine (1770-1837). Botanist. Brother of Sir Edward Sabine (1788-1883) who was interested in terrestrial magnetism.

[38] Robert Brown (1773-1858). Botanist. Explored the world for four years with Capt Matthew Flinders. Librarian to Sir Joseph Banks. Fellow of the Royal Society 1810. Keeper of Botany, British Museum 1827.

[39] Charles Babbage (1791-1871). Son of Benjamin Babbage of the banking firm of Praed, Mackworth and Babbage. Trinity College, Cambridge 1811. Founder with Herschel and others of the 'Analytical Society' for promoting 'the principles of pure D-ism in opposition to the Dot-age of the University' 1812. Invented the 'difference machine' an early form of calculator. FRS 1817. In his latter years 'he considered that one-fourth of his entire working power had been destroyed by audible nuisance'. His son Herschel Babbage went to settle in Adelaide, Australia in 1851.

[40] Thomas Bowdler (1754-1825) Graduated MD 1776. FRS 1781. Lived at the Rhyddings, near Swansea with his wife Harriet 1810-25. Edited the *Family Shakespeare*, removing all those parts considered unsuitable for the Victorian mind, 1818. Hence the term 'to bowdlerize.' After Bowdler's death Lewis Weston Dillwyn purchased Bowdler's own copy.

[41] *Hortus Collinsonianus*, Swansea 1843, unpublished. Copy in the author's collection.

[42] Sir Roderick Impey Murchison (1792-1871). Scottish geologist. Established the Silurian system 1835. Murchison Falls, Uganda and Murchison River, Western Australia are named after him.

[43] One such item recovered from the rubbish heap was a Diary kept by Emma as a child.

[44] *Oestremure*, John Dillwyn Llewelyn,1840s; unpublished. Copy in the author's collection.

[45] Alfred Janson, married Sarah Musgrave Dillwyn, sister of Lewis Weston Dillwyn 1825. In his marriage certificate Mr Janson was described as an underwriter of Walthamstow. Their descendants include Monsignor Ronald Knox, Dillwyn Knox, one of the team responsible for cracking the German Enigma code in the 1939-45 war, and Penelope Fitzgerald, a Booker Prize author.

[46] Now called *Passiflora manicata*; a red-blossomed passion flower.

[47] Loddiges was a family-run nursery garden in Hackney, London, where they grew tropical plants for the first time outside their native habitats. George Loddiges (1786-1846) FLS,FZS,FHS,FMS was a friend of Lewis Weston Dillwyn. For a detailed account of the business see *Loddiges of Hackney*, David Solman, (Hackney Society, 1995).

[48] George Gardener. Born in Glasgow. Trained under William Jackson Hooker when Hooker was in Glasgow, twenty years before the latter went to Kew. Collected in Brazil, Ceylon etc. Information supplied by Jennifer Woods, Royal Botanic Garden, Edinburgh.

[49] Royal Botanic Gardens Kew, Director's correspondence Vol 8 1835-6 letter 52.

[50] Robert H Schomburgk (1804-65). Botanist and explorer. Author of books including *Twelve Views in the Interior of Guiana*, 1841.

[51] *Some Account of an Orchideous House*, John Dillwyn Llewelyn, in the first *Journal of the Horticultural Society* 1846 pp.5-8.

[52] Letter to the author 23 March 1990.

[53] Letter to the author 2 April 1990.

[54] *Victorian Gardens*, Dr Brent Elliott (B T Batsford, London 1986).

[55] Sir Charles Wheatstone (1802-75). English physicist, born in Gloucester. Professor of Experimental Philosophy, Kings College, London 1837. Designed an early stereoscope and also the concertina.

[56] *The Pre-Raphaelite Camera – aspects of Victorian Photography*, Michael Bartram, (Weidenfeld and Nicolson, London 1985).

[57] Letter sold at Sotheby's, London, date unknown. It was recently re-auctioned and purchased by Hans Kraus Jr HonFRPS, of New York, a leading dealer and collector.

[58] *Penllergare Heritage Landscape*, Phase One Report submitted by John Brown & Co and Landskip and Prospect to the Welsh Historic Gardens Trust and others (1993).

[59] A somewhat smaller lake was proposed as part of the planning agreements for housing development.

[60] Penllergaer [*sic*] is Entry No. PGW (Gm) 54 (SWA) in the Cadw/ICOMOS Register of Landscapes, Parks and Gardens of Special Historic Interest in Wales.

**THE DILLWYN FAMILY TREE**

William DILLWYN - Sarah FULLER
m. 1687

John - 1.Mercy PEARCE. 2. Susanna PAINTER

Elizabeth

George - Sarah HILL
1738-1820 m.1759

Lydia

John

**William** - 1. Sarah LOGAN
1743-1824

John - Ann COX

**2. Sarah WESTON**
**m. 1777**

Susanna

Susanna - Samuel EMLEN
1769-1819

John Crook
1780-1

George-Sarah GOWING
1787-?

Judith Nicholls-Paul BEVAN
1781-1868  m:1831

Ann-R D ALEXANDER
1783-1863

Lydia-John SIMS
1785-?

Sarah-Alfred JANSON
1790-?

descendants include Msgnr
Ronald Knox & Penelope
Fitzgerald

John

**Lewis Weston-Mary ADAMS**
**1778-1855 | 1788-1865**

William
1812-19

Lewis Llewelyn-Bessie DE LA BECHE
1814-92

Mary-Revd.M E WELBY
1816-1906

Sarah
1818-28

issue including Amy 1845-1935

Fanny-Matthew MOGGRIDGE
1808-1894

**John-Emma Thomasina TALBOT**
**1810-82      1808-81**

Thereza - Nevil Story MASKELYNE
1834-1926

**John Talbot-Caroline Julia HICKS BEACH**
**1836-1927                    d.1917**

William
1838-66

Emma Charlotte-Henry CRICHTON
1837-1928                    d.1889

Sybella
b.d.1842

Elinor Amy
1844-87

Lucy Caroline
1846-1920

82

# FAMILY TREE TO SHOW RELATIONSHIP WITH TALBOT AND ILCHESTER FAMILIES

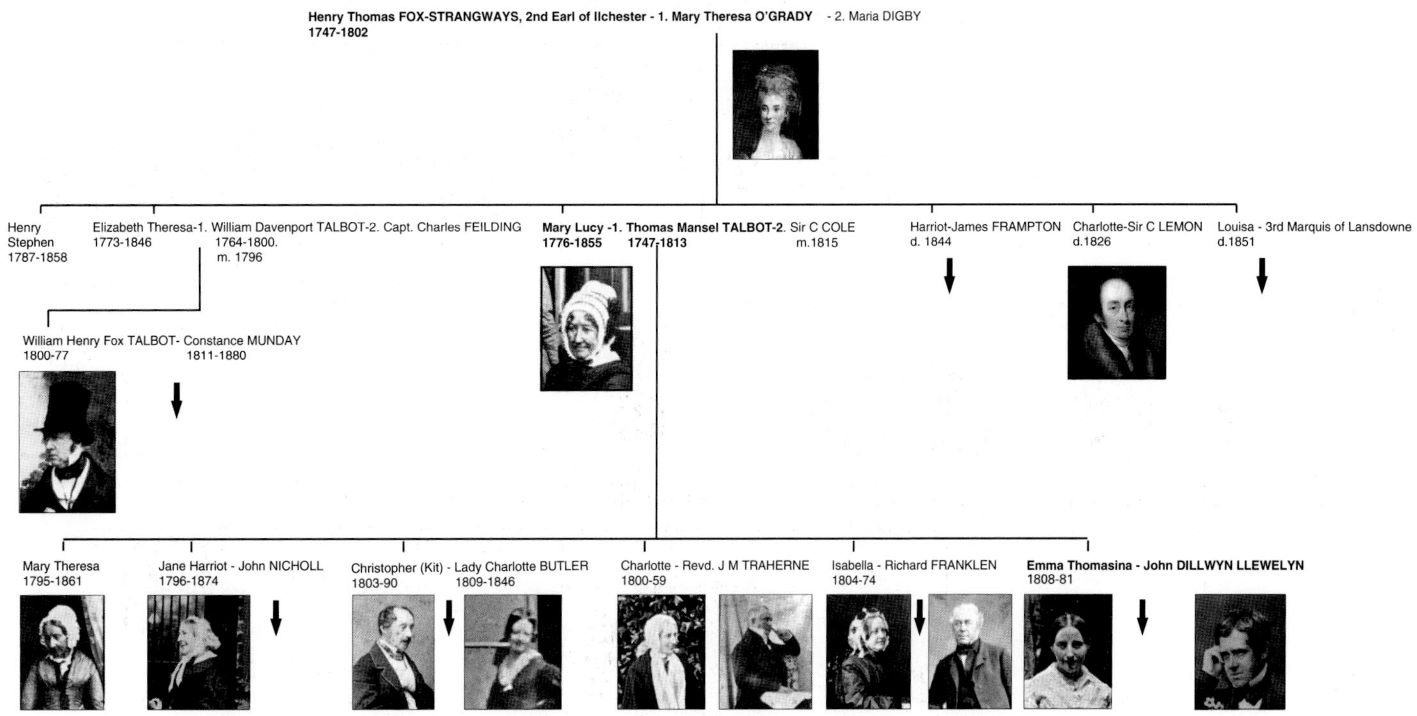

Henry Thomas FOX-STRANGWAYS, 2nd Earl of Ilchester - 1. Mary Theresa O'GRADY   - 2. Maria DIGBY
1747-1802

Henry
Stephen
1787-1858

Elizabeth Theresa-1. William Davenport TALBOT-2. Capt. Charles FEILDING
1773-1846        1764-1800.
                  m. 1796

William Henry Fox TALBOT- Constance MUNDAY
1800-77                    1811-1880

Mary Lucy -1. Thomas Mansel TALBOT-2. Sir C COLE
1776-1855      1747-1813            m.1815

Harriot-James FRAMPTON
d. 1844

Charlotte-Sir C LEMON
d.1826

Louisa - 3rd Marquis of Lansdowne
d.1851

Mary Theresa
1795-1861

Jane Harriot - John NICHOLL
1796-1874

Christopher (Kit) - Lady Charlotte BUTLER
1803-90                1809-1846

Charlotte - Revd. J M TRAHERNE
1800-59

Isabella - Richard FRANKLEN
1804-74

Emma Thomasina - John DILLWYN LLEWELYN
1808-81

THE LAKESIDE – OPPOSITE THE SHANTY. 1853. John Dillwyn Llewelyn.